JUDGMENT, DECISION-MAKING, AND EMBODIED CHOICES

Dear Jessica,

enjoy

Toronto 2023

JUDGMENT, DECISION-MAKING, AND EMBODIED CHOICES

MARKUS RAAB

Institute of Psychology, German Sport University Cologne, Cologne, Germany
School of Applied Sciences, London South Bank University, London, United Kingdom

ACADEMIC PRESS

An imprint of Elsevier

Academic Press
125 London Wall, London EC2Y 5AS, United Kingdom
525 B Street, Suite 1650, San Diego, CA 92101, United States
50 Hampshire Street, 5th Floor, Cambridge, MA 02139, United States
The Boulevard, Langford Lane, Kidlington, Oxford OX5 1GB, United Kingdom

Notices
Knowledge and best practice in this field are constantly changing. As new research and experience
broaden our understanding, changes in research methods, professional practices, or medical
treatment may become necessary.

Practitioners and researchers must always rely on their own experience and knowledge in evaluating
and using any information, methods, compounds, or experiments described herein. In using such
information or methods they should be mindful of their own safety and the safety of others, including
parties for whom they have a professional responsibility.

To the fullest extent of the law, neither the Publisher nor the authors, contributors, or editors, assume
any liability for any injury and/or damage to persons or property as a matter of products liability,
negligence or otherwise, or from any use or operation of any methods, products, instructions, or ideas
contained in the material herein.

Library of Congress Cataloging-in-Publication Data
A catalog record for this book is available from the Library of Congress

British Library Cataloguing-in-Publication Data
A catalogue record for this book is available from the British Library

ISBN: 978-0-12-823523-2

For information on all Academic Press publications
visit our website at https://www.elsevier.com/books-and-journals

Publisher: Nikki Levy
Senior Acquisitions Editor: Joslyn Chaiprasert-Paguio
Editorial Project Manager: Billie Jean Fernandez
Production Project Manager: Niranjan Bhaskaran
Senior Cover designer: Victoria Pearson

Typeset by SPi Global, India

Working together
to grow libraries in
developing countries

www.elsevier.com • www.bookaid.org

To my mother
Erdmute Karla-Herma Johanna Raab
(16 March 1946–19 November 2018)

Contents

Preface   xi
Acknowledgments   xiii
Blurb   xv

1. What are embodied choices?   1

A definition of embodied choices   2
Embodied choices as gut feelings   3
This book   7
References   8

2. Simple heuristics—How we make decisions   9

**3. Embodied cognition—How our bodies and movements
     shape our thinking   13**

4. How the body and the environment affect our thinking?   29

Movements influence our emotional judgments   32
How do gut feelings lead to embodied choices?   35
How do the gut and brain work together?   38
How does the gut change your decisions?   41
How does the gut affect your risky behavior?   41
References   44

**5. Action enables perception and cognition and thus embodied
     choices   47**

Actions enable social interactions   52
Do muscles have intelligence? The case of motor intentionality   56
Embodied choices influenced by the environment   58
References   61

6. Decisions when moving your mind   65

Esthetic embodied choices   67
Sounds and embodied choices   68
How to we predict intentions of others and generate different options
to choose from?   70

Vestibular signals, touch, and embodied choices   72
Movement in high-stakes decisions   74
References   75

7. Embodied choices in real life   77

Medical decisions   77
Shopping decisions   79
Liking people   80
Liking objects   81
References   83

8. Individual and cultural differences in embodied choices   85

Do women and left-handers have better intuition?   87
Embodied higher cognitive functions   88
Embodied choices when multitasking   94
When does the body malfunction and how do choices change
as a result?   97
Embodied choices in making financial and health decisions   103
References   109

9. How do you choose when it is your first time?   113

Climate choices   114
Moral embodied choices   115
References   116

10. Where do embodied choices come from?   119

11. How can embodied choices be trained?   125

Embodied choices in educational settings   126
Learning embodied choices   127
Using intuition to predict sports outcomes   129
Using tools in embodied choices   130
Using implicit learning to improve embodied choices   134
Changing the environment or adapting to it   135
References   136

12.   How to cope with uncertainty in COVID-19 times   139

How do we now rate the actions of governments regarding health
measures for society and individuals?   142
References   144

**13.   Ten statements for simplifying your life with embodied
choices   145**

#1: Choices are embodied choices   145
#2: Choices are governed by a less-is-more strategy   146
#3: Choices are grounded in your movements   146
#4: Actions enable perception and cognition   147
#5: Decisions are influenced by your long-term movement history   148
#6: Choices in the real environment can change the impact of the body   148
#7: Embodied choices are individualized and culture dependent   149
#8: First-time choices can be made embodied   150
#9: Embodied choices are tuned by evolution   150
#10: Embodied choices can be trained   151

Index   *153*

Preface

This book focuses on judgment and decision-making from an embodied cognition perspective that is how our bodies influence how we think, decide, and act. I coined the term embodied choices for the fact that indeed the body plays a major role in our daily choices, even often as an unnoticed player. Understanding judgment and decision-making without being embodied has been advanced mainly in isolation within cognitive psychology, and the movement science played no role. Recently, this has changed. Rather than viewing observable actions as merely the outcome of some mental processes the bidirectional interactions of mind and body as a coherent system became a new paradigm in cognitive sciences.

The book is structured in 13 chapters that use scientific findings on how people decide in daily situations, lab experiments spanning from millisecond, based on our intuitions or long-term decisions, from whom to marry to what to do next in life. In simple words, examples from research as well as individual or group choices are presented to explain how our movements, our current body postures, or our gut feelings affect our choices. Examples will cover decisions based on experience and when we make them the first time. I hope that this book will increase our acknowledgment of embodied choices and how to trust them.

Acknowledgments

This book would have been impossible without the dignity of researchers in the whole world to share their thinking and results in studies of embodied choice, and the many participants providing us with the insights by their choices. I am thankful for the support provided by the Department of Performance Psychology and the German Sport University in Cologne, Germany, for allowing me a sabbatical to travel and write this book. Previous and current members of the Department of Performance Psychology have been incredibly important in developing the main ideas of how the body shapes its mind. I would like to thank my hosts during my sabbatical travel: Miki Bar-Eli and Ronnie Lidor at Wingate, Israel; my colleagues at the London South Bank University, UK; Clare MacMahon at LaTrobe University; Rich Masters and colleagues at Waikato University New Zealand; and Joe Johnson, Miami University, USA. I also thank Anita Todd and Billie Jean Fernandez, the Elsevier publisher team for editing. I convey my thanks to Daniela Kauschke for helping me with the figures in the book.

Finally, I extend my sincere thanks to my son Lukas, my wife Marei, and the rest of our gang—Mia, Emily, Bo, and Leo as well our dogs Peluche and Dara.

In this enthralling book, Markus Raab argues that good decisions require that mind and body work together. Having worked with sports players for decades, Raab knows first-hand that clever decisions are about movement and timing—and not just in sports. This lively, well-written, and innovative book provides striking examples of embodied choice, conscious, and unconscious. It shows how smart heuristics exploit bodily coordination, and it reminds us of the importance of gut feelings when making high-stake decisions. Highly recommended.

Gerd Gigerenzer
Max Planck Institute for Human Development, Berlin, Germany

CHAPTER ONE

What are embodied choices?

I like spaghetti Bolognese. I do not remember when I first realized I like it or why—I simply do. When I did my PhD at the University of Heidelberg in Germany, next to our offices was a student cafe offering spaghetti Bolognese every day. I was in paradise! Well after 2 weeks of daily choosing my preferred option I tried something else. I guess I was fed up with spaghetti, or the other options sounded good as well. Or maybe I just wanted the cashier to change her facial expression, which usually telegraphed "again"? Often, it is not so easy to give a reason (or many) for our choices.

Let us change this story slightly and instead of choosing food, consider being given a daily choice of either Lottery X with Option A of winning 10 euros for sure and Option B with a 10% probability of winning 50 euros or Lottery Y with Option A of winning 5 euros for sure and Option B with a 10% probability of winning 25 euros (Fig. 1).

Most reasonable people would choose Lottery X over Y. People would choose that option forever if presented daily. This is in contrast to the food choice I presented earlier. If you asked them why, they would most likely say "10 euros for sure is twice as much as the 5 euros in Lottery Y" or "a 10% probability of winning 50 euros versus 25 euros makes Lottery X more attractive." Whether you choose the risky option in each lottery or pick the sure option may depend on personal factors or the current situation, and we will discuss this later. Often when I ask people, for example, how they decided to change jobs, they tell me why they chose to do so, such as dissatisfaction with the previous job or better personal development and career opportunity in the new job. I often need to repeat the question because what I want to know is *how* they processed their two options, that is, staying or leaving. I explain this by asking them to best describe all their experiences, feelings, and thoughts at the time they made the decision. I ask them also how they decided whom to ask for advice and what information and tools, for example, paper and pencil, they used when they were deciding; I asked them whether they were sometimes in favor of one option and sometimes in favor of the other, and what about the situation differed when preferring one or the other. Some people kept on explaining the why

Judgment, Decision-Making, and Embodied Choices
https://doi.org/10.1016/B978-0-12-823523-2.00001-5

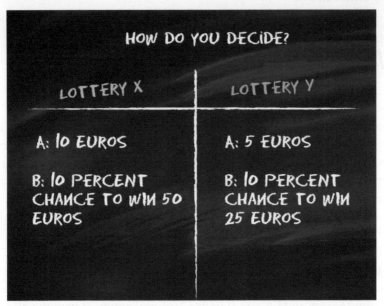

Fig. 1 Which lottery would you choose? Within each lottery, which option would you choose?

and listing all their reasons, whereas I was still interested in the how, and especially one key question: Could there be some difference in their bodily state that explains some of the changes in preferences or feelings about the choice options, all else being equal? In short, I wondered if the decision to change jobs is actually an embodied choice.

A definition of embodied choices

Simple heuristics are rules of thumb that are useful when limited time and resources force people to decide quickly between two or more options, often on the basis of limited information. Yet researchers who explore decisions in the real world have so far neglected one important cue: the human body and its stored sensorimotor experiences. In accordance with Lepora and Pezzulo's simple definition of perceptual decision-making, that actions are a part of the decision-making process [1], an *embodied choice* can be defined as one in which the sensorimotor system itself has provided information to aid in making the decision. For example, in basketball, shooting performance has been shown to correlate with dynamic visual acuity [2], the perceptual ability to resolve details in dynamic situations of moving players and objects. If the dynamic visual acuity changes due to fatigue or other factors, the particular change may serve as a cue when making the decision to pass or shoot. Other cues often used to explain people's choices refer to cost-value analysis and cognitive examination of complex calculations of expected values, but these seem to be less important [1].

For embodied choices, the motor execution of an option is thus not only the end product of a cognitive choice between two options but also serves as a cue about whether one or the other option can be processed [3]. An important implication is that it is assumed that choosing what to do and how to do it happen sequentially, in two phases. However, it seems likely that these processes run in parallel, as supported by neurophysiological and animal research [4]. In short, and in the words of Koziol and colleagues, "We were not born to think. We were born to move." (p. 11) [5]. In embodied choices the evolutionarily much older bodily functions are used to embody choices.

Embodied choices as gut feelings

When you are looking at the array of choices in the student cafe, your body may signal you that it wants something other than your usual lunch; in salary negotiations, your cognitive system tells you simply more money is better. But are these things true? Using intuition for your choices is often called relying on "gut feelings," and recent research indicates that many choices are indeed made in what some researchers call the second brain: the gut.

In the last decade, it has been shown that the gut can influence choices in business and many decisions in daily life beyond what to have for lunch. Here is one example: Judges' decisions on the bench were analyzed to determine whether they were made before or after lunch and whether they were in favor of the accused or not [6]. Judges were found to be more lenient in their court judgments after lunch compared with before lunch. This is surprising given that cases are assigned to their position on the docket independent of anything that should influence the decision. One explanation that the study put forward was that the activation of the gut after lunch influenced the decisions, but how?

In the last decades, researchers have found impressive evidence that indeed, the brain-gut behavior connection is stronger than previously thought [7]. In contrast to the study of judges in court, many recent experiments have manipulated the gut in controlled laboratory experiments to test how changes in the gut influence choices. To illustrate, in a study by Schmidt and colleagues from the University of Oxford in the United Kingdom [8], daily ingestion of probiotics (fructooligosaccharides or Bimuno galactooligosaccharides) for 3 weeks reduced the waking cortisol response and changed vigilance reaction times in an attentional dot-probe task (Fig. 2).

This is a task in which participants' attention is measured by simply showing them pairs of faces, one with emotional valence and one neutral, presented in different locations on a computer screen, followed by a small visual probe (a dot) appearing in the location vacated by one of these. Participants are required to indicate the location of the probe as quickly as possible without compromising on accuracy. Response latencies on the task provide a "snapshot" of the distribution of the participants' attention: They respond faster to probes presented in the attended relative to the unattended location. For example, attentional bias (i.e., the tendency to attend to one stimulus more than another) to threat is evident when participants respond faster to probes that replace a threat-related stimulus than probes that replace a neutral one. The reverse pattern indicates threat-related attentional avoidance. Importantly the probiotic effect was not found in the control placebo condition (ingestion of maltodextrin). It is too early for generalization, but a recent overview of related studies suggests that changing the gut state causally influences human behavior [9].

How one explains gut feelings or other choices simply depends on the theory applied. This in itself is a choice from an array of, as of this writing, 264 theories that have been developed. In a book [10] I wrote with Henning Plessner, a colleague working in Heidelberg, Germany, and Michael Bar-Eli, a colleague working in Israel Beer-Sheva, we showed that the choice of a specific decision-making theory influences how a researcher explains a choice (this book will not go through all of them but will highlight those that are meaningful for the applications discussed). Let me illustrate this with a famous choice to show how the expected outcome and explanations change depending on the theory applied: In the Natural History Museum in London, there is a note penned by Charles Darwin about whether to marry. Darwin listed the pros and cons in a table—arguments in favor of marriage on the left, such as having children, constant companionship, and having someone to be one's beloved, and reasons not to marry on the right, such as freedom to go where one likes, "choice of Society and little of it," conversation with "clever men at clubs," and not being forced to see relatives. After compiling the list and counting more items against marriage,

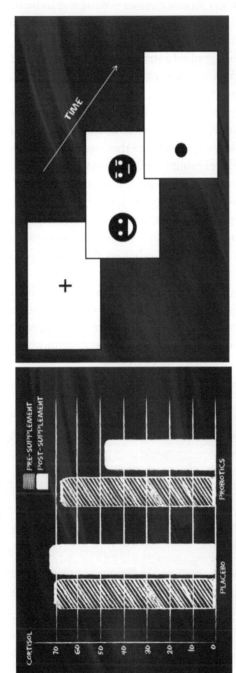

Fig. 2 (A) Cortisol response presupplement and postsupplement for people taking a placebo versus probiotics. (B) Task that starts with a fixation *cross*, a *visual face* that is positive or neutral, and then a *dot* is presented, participants are asked to respond to its location.

he wrote QED (*quod erat demonstrandum*—what was to be shown) and married his cousin Emma, had 10 children with her, and developed his theory of natural selection, which remains widely accepted.

Well, if Darwin had applied a strategy in which he would have added up the pros and cons and chosen the option with the most items this would have led to the decision not to marry, as there were more items against than in favor. But he might have assigned weights to the items with the so-called weighted-additive strategy, giving positive items more weight (i.e., value) than negative items, leading to a choice that favored marriage when the sums were totaled. Finally a very simple rule of thumb could explain the choice as well, such as the elimination-by-aspects heuristic that says if one option has an important item and the other does not, delete the second option from the choice set. For example, if having children was very important to Darwin— and in his day having children outside the marriage was rare and socially unacceptable—when deciding whether to marry he would ignore all the other items except having children (Fig. 3).

What is true for marriages seem to hold as well for other choices, such as choosing desserts, by arguing that intuition trumps deliberation [11]. In a study at Harvard University, Inbar and colleagues argued that one might have an intuitive sense that one dessert is better than another, but verbalizing

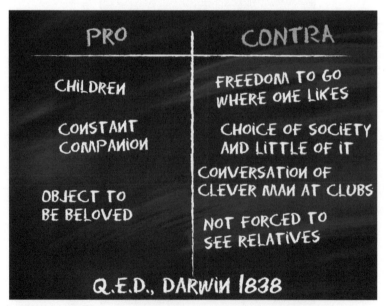

Fig. 3 Darwin's decision table for deciding to marry his cousin Emma.

the choice is quite hard compared to other tasks. One reason that verbalizing some of our choices is that they are intuitive and at the moment decided. Researchers tried to influence whether persons choose by intuition or deliberation. For example, when Inbar asked students not about desserts but about waste dump this is what happened: They asked students in which of two cities they would locate a toxic waste dump. Interestingly, they used a large set of choices and asked whether the students would rely on their intuition and it seems that people use rational thinking for some choices, such as medical treatments, military tactics, or waste dump in this example, much more than others, such as choosing desserts or spouses.

Many of these daily or rare-but-important decisions are based on simple heuristics. I am a strong proponent of the simple heuristics account, so you will hear more about it than other strategies, but as I argued earlier, how one frames decision-making is a choice in itself, and you can make your own choice after I have contrasted the heuristics with other proposals.

An important distinction is made in the Darwin's example: Do you follow your intuition or your reflective thinking? This difference has been discussed by many, such as the Nobel laureate Daniel Kahneman in his book *Thinking, Fast and Slow* [12], and is the key feature of all so-called dual-process models of decision making. However, the process is the opposite of that in Darwin's case: A first impression on the idea to marry as an intuitive judgment that comes before the analysis. For Darwin, intuition came after the analysis. Dual-process models suggest using intuition and reflection, but how those processes interaction is often a matter of debate in science. We will come back to this distinction between intuition and reflection and when and how it is useful to describe and explain choices.

This book

Judgment, Decision-Making, and Embodied Choices encompasses 13 chapters. In this chapter, I have defined embodied choices. Chapter 2 shows how simple heuristics explain how we decide. Chapter 3 introduces the concept of embodied cognition that is how our bodies and movements shape our thinking. Chapter 4 covers how the mind is influenced by the body and its movements and likewise how our bodies and the environment shape our thinking. Chapter 5 provides more evidence that bodily positions and movements influence how we see and think. Chapter 6 presents the obvious application, that is, sports. Chapter 7 investigates daily-life decisions that often involve cost-benefit trade-offs and uncertainty. Chapter 8 shows that the body plays a role in higher cognitive processes such as problem-solving and creativity. Chapter 9 brings the body to the forefront in societal decisions, such as those addressing climate change and many others. Chapter 10 provides information on how embodied choices evolve. Chapter 11 covers how to train embodied choices. Chapter 12 covers a health crisis taken place in spring 2020 and provides information how to cope with uncertainty and to educate risk-literacy. Finally, Chapter 13 focuses on the takeaway message: how your life includes embodied choices.

References

[1] N.F. Lepora, G. Pezzulo, Embodied choice: how action influences perceptual decision making. PLoS Comput. Biol. 11 (4) (2015) e1004110, https://doi.org/10.1371/journal.pcbi.1004110.

[2] R.P. Beals, A. Mayyasi, A.E. Templeton, W.L. Johnston, The relationship between basketball shooting performance and certain visual attributes, Am. J. Optom. Arch. Am. Acad. Optom. 48 (1971) 585–590.

[3] B.L. Connors, R. Rende, Embodied decision-making style: below and beyond cognition. Front. Psychol. 9 (2018) 1123, https://doi.org/10.3389/fpsyg.2018.01123.

[4] P. Cisek, A. Pastor-Bernier, On the challenges and mechanisms of embodied decisions, Philos. Trans. R. Soc. Lond. Ser. B Biol. Sci. 369 (2014) 20130479. https://doi.org/10.1098/rstb.2013.0479.

[5] F. Leonhard, D. Koziol, E. Budding, D. Chidekel, From movement to thought: executive function, embodied cognition and the cerebellum. Cerebellum (2001) https://doi.org/10.1007/s12311-011-0321-y.

[6] S. Danziger, J. Levav, L. Avnaim-Pesso, Extraneous factors in judicial decisions, Proc. Natl. Acad. Sci. 108 (17) (2011) 6889–6892.

[7] J.F. Cryan, K.J. O'Riordan, C.S.M. Cowan, K.V. Sandhu, T.F.S. Bastiaanssen, M. Boehme, M.G. Codagnone, S. Cussotto, C. Fulling, A.V. Golubeva, K.E. Guzzetta, M. Jaggar, C.M. Long-Smith, J.M. Lyte, J.A. Martin, A. Molinero-Perez, G. Moloney, E. Morelli, E. Morillas, R. O'Connor, J.S. Cruz-Pereira, V.L. Peterson, K. Rea, N.L. Ritz, E. Sherwin, S. Spichak, E.M. Teichman, M. van de Wouw, A.P. Ventura-Silva, S.E. Wallace-Fitzsimons, N. Hyland, G. Clarke, T.G. Dinan, The microbiota-gut-brain axis. Physiol. Rev. 99 (2019) 1877–2013, https://doi.org/10.1152/physrev.00018.2018.

[8] K. Schmidt, et al., Prebiotic intake reduces the waking cortisol response and alters emotional bias in healthy volunteers, Psychopharmacology 232 (2015) 1793–1801.

[9] E.A. Mayers, Gut feelings. The emerging biology of gut-brain communication. Nat. Neurosci. 12 (2011) 453–466, https://doi.org/10.1038/nrn3071.

[10] M. Bar-Eli, Boost!: How the Psychology of Sports Can Enhance Your Performance in Management and Work, Oxford University Press, Oxford, UK, 2018.

[11] Y. Inbar, J. Cone, T. Gilovich, People's intuitions about intuitive insight and intuitive choice, J. Pers. Soc. Psychol. 99 (2010) 232.

[12] D. Kahneman, Thinking, Fast and Slow, Farrar, Straus and Giroux, New York, 2011.

CHAPTER TWO

Simple heuristics—How we make decisions

How humans make decisions is one of the most important problems faced by people who want to help decision-makers to make good choices in a variety of situations. Humans have limited time and cognitive resources, and sometimes the information is missing, so we need to rely on shortcuts, that is, rules of thumb, or as certain scientists would say, we need to apply simple heuristics.

Here is an example: If you have never heard of "simple heuristics," you simply Google the phrase, right? Google will display 16 million hits in less than half a second. You will search from top to bottom, stop your search when you find a link that sounds as if it will satisfy your need, and then click on it to access the information. No one would start by searching all the links or start from the very last entry in a large list (if you do this, you need help). We use a simple search strategy that rarely takes us beyond the first page of a large search list, as we know that Google sorts the entries using some matching algorithm. We do not know exactly how this algorithm works and sometimes we ignore the first entries as they are marked as advertisements and do not always reflect the best fit.

Using a quick-and-dirty Google search is not an optimal choice as we may miss out on important and maybe even more relevant information, but we are regularly satisfied with such a short and often the best cursory check. Optimization is often not humanly possible. And indeed, even computers filter information and restrict their search routines according to the amount of information available. For example, only recently chess computers began to win against the best human players by no longer calculating all possible moves and predicting all possible combinations of specific moves and follow-ups until a game ends. Even the best computers runs multiple search routines in parallel cannot process that number of calculations in a short time. If you want to see how one of the best human chess players perceived this change, I recommend the book *Deep Thinking* by the world champion Garry Kasparov, who is well known for his strategic play. Not all chess players equally trust their intuitions. For example, in the 2018 chess world championship, Magnus Carlson, who is known to be an intuitive and creative player, won against Fabiano Caruana, who is known to be a deliberative and strategic player, only after the draws in the first phase forced the players to engage in time-pressured games in the second phase, in which the intuitive player naturally gained an advantage.

Under time-pressure, simple heuristics have an advantage because they are fast, and they are fast because they rely on limited information. All the heuristics discussed in this book are structured in the same way using basic building blocks: a search rule (e.g., search Google results starting from the top), a stopping rule (e.g., stop on Page 1 as soon something roughly fits the search criteria), and a decision rule (click on a link and read the entry). As we learn later when "moving your mind," beyond deciding what to do, it is important as well to decide how to do it. Execution rules for performing an action are added to the building blocks when needed.

Let us consider a very simple heuristic, the recognition heuristic: It simply states that if you have two options and you recognize one but not the other, choose the one you recognize. Advertisements prime the recognition heuristic: When choosing from an array of products or services, you may take the one you recognize from an advertisement. The recognition heuristic can also be used when a person has some knowledge. Have you heard of "Who Wants to Be a Millionaire," the popular television game show that ran for many years? Contestants had to answer a series of multiple choice questions. Correct answers allowed the contestant to progress to the next level and play for more money; contestants could stop before answering something wrong and keep their winnings up to that point, but an incorrect answer meant the end of that contestant's run and forfeiture of all money earned. Here is a question that is typical of the game (for simplification, only two options instead of the game's four options): Which city has more inhabitants? (A) Kyoto or (B) Fukuoka. Well if you are like me, you recognize only one of them—Kyoto   and vote for that. Fukuoka is not as well known by most people outside Asia, but actually it has only a few less inhabitants than Kyoto. Do people rely on the recognition heuristic in such cases? It seems they do, as researchers in Berlin have shown for many sets of city comparisons. Of course, if you recognize neither of them or both of them you cannot apply the recognition heuristic, and this sometimes explains why too much of knowledge can even hinder making the correct choice. In the task just described, for example, Germans have been more often correct in identifying American cities in comparison with Americans, who have more experiences of American cities stored in episodic memory, having perhaps visited them or come across them in school [1,2].

But how do we know that the participants relied on the recognition heuristic and did not simply guess or recognize both but still decided on Kyoto? Assessing participants' recognition of these cities before or after the experiment is one strategy that has been applied, as well as scanning their brains: Functional magnetic resonance imaging has been used to show that the brain does respond to recognition and applies the recognition heuristic [3]. Why is applying the recognition heuristic often considered as a good choice? Well, that you recognize one city and not the other is not purely random: Larger cities tend to appear more often in the news or on the Internet or are more likely to have been visited by many people, and indeed the correlation between a city's size and its appearance in the news is positive and has been shown to exist quite frequently [2]. Of course, you can find counterexamples indicating that using the recognition heuristic leads to an incorrect decision. Information or cues, as researchers from the simple heuristics camp call information, can be quantified by the number of times a decision using the cue was correct. This indicates what is called *cue validity*. Cue validity tells you how much you can trust the cue to be helpful. Some cues are not reliable at all. If you have ever watched a soccer game and seen the ball go out at the sideline you would have seen players of both teams gesturing to claim the ball's possession. Referees ignore such hand waving because it is not at all indicative of who should possess the ball.

Let us consider a more serious matter: health. When I was playing volleyball in my glory days I had an ACL (anterior cruciate ligament) injury on the right knee, and the doctor offered me (and my mom) two surgical options of different degrees of complexity. In one option, they would operate to fix the damaged meniscus and the ACL, and, in the other option, they would take a part of the ligament of the quadriceps (large upper leg muscle) and replace my damaged knee ligament to make the new ligament structure stronger. I was 15 and simply wanted to resume playing volleyball as quickly as possible. My mom wanted a safe operation and no long-term damage to my body. We both, however, used a simple "trust the doc" heuristic. We asked what he would do if it was his child in a similar situation, and he recommended the second operation for the long-term sport activities, even if the recovery was longer because the knee is more stable for sports such as volleyball. The trade-off was that I missed the youth championship, but I was able to play for years following. Even today, when I feel a little twinge in my right knee while paddling on my stand up paddle board I wonder what would have happened if I had opted for the first operation.

Although using specific strategies can make choices better, choices are not always clearly good or bad. For example, unlike inferences such as which of two cities is larger, where there is a correct, factual answer, food, music, or art preferences can hardly be categorized as good or bad. Both preferences and inferences have received much attention in decision-making research, with many researchers interested in the errors and biased decisions that people make. The current list of so-called cognitive biases in Wikipedia [4] ends only after scrolling a long way down (we will discover some of these biases later). For some researchers, simple heuristics are short cuts that are prone to produce errors as they ignore information and are fast. However, as other researchers have indicated that using heuristics does not always lead to errors and biased decisions, as I show; it seems we use them in an adaptive way to compensate for our limited knowledge or limited resources, such as the time we have to decide.

In the following chapters, I illustrate the way the body makes us smarter through the use of embodied choices, or at least affects our thinking. I talk about simple perception tasks, gesturing, and thinking about space or time. How gut feelings are actually based on microbiota activations and how this changes our thinking is stressed as well.

References

[1] G. Gigerenzer, D. Goldstein, Reasoning the fast and frugal way: models of bounded rationality, Cogn. Sci. 103 (1996) 650–666.
[2] G. Gigerenzer, P.M. Todd, The ABC Research Group, Simple Heuristics That Make Us Smart, Oxford University Press, New York, 1999.
[3] K.G. Volz, L.J. Schooler, R.I. Schubotz, M. Raab, G. Gigerenzer, D.Y. von Cramon, Why you think Milan is larger than Modena: neural correlates of the recognition heuristic, J. Cogn. Neurosci. 18 (11) (2006) 1924–1936.
[4] https://en.wikipedia.org/wiki/List_of_cognitive_biases.

CHAPTER THREE

Embodied cognition—How our bodies and movements shape our thinking

Embodied cognition [1] as a research topic is as old as I am. A typical Wikipedia definition goes like this: "Embodied cognition is the theory that many features of cognition, whether human or otherwise, are shaped by aspects of the entire body of the organism" [2].

In the past 50 years, more than 13,000 articles are listed in the research databases such as Web of Science on the general topic of embodiment that tries to understand how our bodies and movements shape our thinking. In words of the late Ether Thelen from Indiana University about 20 years ago:

> *To say that cognition is embodied means that it arises from bodily interactions with the world. From this point of view, cognition depends on the kinds of experiences that come from having a body with particular perceptual and motor capabilities that are inseparably linked and that together form the matrix within which reasoning, memory, emotion, language, and all other aspects of mental life are meshed [3].*

As the quote by Esther Thelen vividly puts it, the term embodied cognition describes a perspective on the human being that assumes substantial interactions between cognition, perception, and movement. A logical consequence of this interaction is that these three cannot be considered independent of each other. In contrast to classic, amodal cognition theories, which consider the brain to be the central governor of mental representations and cognition, embodied cognition approaches postulate that thought processes are not independent of perception and movement processes but are embodied in a multimodal manner. From this assumption, it follows that thought processes do not exist exclusively as internal processes in the head but consist of interactions between the body of an individual (and its abilities and skills) and the environment as Mark Rowlands from the University of Miami in 2010 puts it nicely [4]. Consequently, from an embodied cognition perspective, the brain is the only one part of a broader action system that generates solutions for tasks from all three elements combined: cognition, perception, and movement. You may remember the example from Chapter 1: How does an outfielder catch a fly ball? I introduced a simple solution using a simple heuristic approach that was different from classical information processing theories of decision-making. If we now use embodied cognition work, we can see that the body will help us to make such decisions when we integrate different perception, movement, and cognition in contrast to amodal theories that separate all these processes. Amodal cognitive theories would say that the outfielder visually perceives the fly ball and its speed, size, direction, and so on, and the brain uses this information to create an internal model that predicts where the ball will land. The brain then sends instructions to the body to move to that location. According to this solution, the optimal movement toward the ball would be a straight line (because people prefer the shortest distance between two things).

Embodied cognition approaches would seek the solution to the out-fielder task by first asking the following question: What resources does the outfielder have to solve the task most efficiently? Yes, the outfielder could build an internal model, but this is a time-consuming and difficult endeavor. The player could likewise use their cognitive, perceptual, and movement capacities in combination, for example, by moving (movement skills) and observing the ball (perceptual skills) with the overall goal (cognitive capacity) of catching it. As soon as the player begins to move, they no longer see the ball first rise and then fall in a parabolic curve. Instead, they sense their own movement and the movement of the flying ball. The player now has several options for adapting their movement to that of the ball and thus getting to the place where the ball will land: One way is to match their running trajectory to the trajectory of the ball so that the trajectories zero each other out and the ball looks as if it is flying in a straight line from the outfielder's point of view. Another possibility would be that instead of adjusting their running trajectory, they adjust their running speed to that of the ball: If the outfielder first runs faster and then slows down as soon as the ball loses speed, then from their perspective the ball looks as if it is moving at a constant speed. Both solutions result in the outfielder being in the right place at exactly the right time to catch the ball. If we compare the solutions of the amodal approach and the embodied cognition approach, it quickly becomes clear that the solutions of the embodied cognition approach are the ones that reflect reality much better (fielders rarely walk in a straight line at constant speed). Which of the two strategies proposed by embodied cognition approaches (adjusting the movement curve or adjusting the speed of movement) is used depends, among other things, on contextual factors [5]. Either way, an embodied cognition perspective can help to explain human behavior in a holistic and efficient way. In combination with the simple heuristics explained in Chapter 1, we will be later able to understand how embodied choices realize complex behaviors.

The idea of a holistic understanding of cognition that encapsulates perception and movement is by no means new and much older than the recent discussions of 50 years about the concept of embodied cognition. Philosophers, especially representatives of phenomenology, laid the foundation for today's embodied cognition approaches. Phenomenologists such as Maurice Merleau-Ponty already in 1945 placed the *experience of the environment* in the foreground. The central question was determining the meaning of objects, events, the self or others, and how this meaning is created through a person's experience and interaction with the environment.

The work of Maurice Merleau-Ponty (1908–61), a French philosopher and one of the most important voices in phenomenology, has had a particular influence on today's embodied cognition approaches. Maurice Merleau-Ponty further developed Edmund Husserl and Martin Heidegger's basic phenomenological ideas by focusing on the body and its perception (corporeality) and calling for the abolition of the classic dichotomous division of the body on the one hand and the soul on the other. In Maurice Merleau-Ponty's own words:

> True reflection presents me to myself not as idle and inaccessible subjectivity, but as identical with my presence in the world and to others, as I am now realizing it: I am all that I see, I am an intersubjective field, not despite my body and historical situation, but, on the contrary, by being this body and this situation, and through them, all the rest [6].

What today's embodied cognition approaches have in common is that they agree in their central assumption: Cognition, perception, and movement processes cannot be considered independent of each other but rather influence and condition each other. Today's embodied cognition approaches differ mainly in terms of the role ascribed to the body. For example, Lawrence Shapiro in 2011 [7] from the University of Wisconsin-Madison distinguished three different perspectives: conceptualization, replacement, and constitution. In the following discussion, I present examples and influential literature for each of the three perspectives. Just one anecdote from my glory days as a student. During my study years, I was once visiting the University of Wisconsin-Madison and took some lectures in psychology and kinesiology. Sitting at Lake Mendota that has the size of catchment area of $562\,\mathrm{km}^2$

or some $217\,\text{mi}^2$ that my own country could nearly be put into, impressed me. I have to admit not as much as my first trip to the United States, when I was at the end of my high school with the International Counselor Exchange program helping socially challenged kids from the Chicago city area for their sport activities during summer camps. Visiting for instance Lake Bomoseen with some 2370 acres and having day trips in a canoe provides a new measure of size for a European boy.

The conceptualization perspective argues, in general terms, that the way we understand the world depends on the shape of our bodies. Conceptualization predicts that differences between different bodies create different conceptualizations of the world. In other words, different bodies perceive different worlds, or lead to different worlds.

An illustrative example is the perception of color. Which colors we perceive and how we perceive them depend on neurophysiological conditions that differ from person to person.

In 2015 an image of a two-colored dress confused users of social networks worldwide: #TheDress. Some saw a black-and-blue-striped dress in the photo, others a white-and-gold-striped dress. How is it possible that the perception of color differs so drastically between different people?

Karl Gegenfurtner and colleagues from the University of Gießen in Germany examined this phenomenon empirically under controlled light conditions. They found that all participants in their experiment saw similar shades of color that differed only in their brightness. The perceived colors ranged from a very bright light blue to a bright medium blue on one side and from a gold to a dark brown on the other side. Both colors of the dress are located in the color circle on the so-called daylight axis: depending on the time of day (or the position of the sun), daylight tends to be bluish (midday) or yellowish (morning and evening). Normally, people unconsciously filter out the influence of this bluish or yellowish light and thus correct for the influence of daylight—but for this they need colors as comparison points that lie outside the daylight axis (such as greenish or reddish shades). These are completely missing in #TheDress and therefore any information about the lighting conditions is missing. The interpretation of the colors depends on the environment in which the dress is situated—it could be a blue dress exposed to warm yellowish light, but it could just as well be a white dress exposed to cool bluish light.

The popular image of the two-colored dress that preoccupied the social networks thus showed in an impressive way that we do not just perceive the pure physical properties through our senses. Rather, we have assumptions about the world that influence our interpretation of sensory stimuli—and these assumptions can be very different across individuals.

A second proposition of the conceptualization perspective is that our ability to form and understand concepts is based on the fact that we move in the world by using our bodies: The concepts of "front" and "back," for example, only make sense to beings who themselves have a front and a back. According to George Lakoff, University of California, and Mark Johnson, University of Oregon: "If all beings on this planet were uniform stationary spheres floating in some medium and perceiving equally in all directions, they would have no concepts of front and back" [8]. Our body with its specific characteristics therefore determines the emergence of concepts as George Lakoff and Mark Johnson would put it. If we take this thought a step further, the question arises whether this also applies to abstract concepts that have no direct relation to our bodies or the sensorimotor experiences made through our bodies (such as our concept of time). According to George Lakoff and Mark Johnson, the answer is yes, because abstract concepts are grounded in concrete concepts that can be perceived with our sensorimotor system. It is assumed, for example, that the abstract concept of time is based on the concrete concept of space: This is reflected, among other things, in our language: "The evening lies before me" is a sentence with temporal information that is expressed with a spatial expression (before). Because in a sport psychological context the connection between movement, time, and space plays an important role, the sport psychological arena is particularly well suited to test predictions from an embodied cognition perspective.

A third proposition of the conceptualization perspective as defined by Lawrence Shapiro in 2011 is an "embodied" response to the "symbol grounding problem" [9]. The symbol grounding problem is about how language acquires meaning for us. A well-known thought experiment is the Chinese room. From an embodied cognition perspective, the answer is that language acquires meaning as soon as we move in the world as embodied agents and interact with it. Without interaction we can learn language, but it remains meaningless.

The Chinese room is a thought experiment demonstrating that human intelligence cannot be simulated by a computer program developed by John Searle 1980. It goes like this: Imagine that a person who does not know Chinese is in a room and is slipped a piece of paper through a gap in the wall to the outside with stories and questions about these stories in Chinese.

The person in the room has a handbook (in a language that the person understands) with instructions on what to say based on the story and the questions. Using the handbook, the person in the room now answers by returning the responses through the gap to the outside. In doing so, the person gives the correct answers but does not understand the answers they are giving. To someone standing outside the room, however, it seems as if the person inside the room is fluent in Chinese. Transferring this argumentation to the Turing test, the conclusion is that a program that passes the Turing test is not necessarily intelligent; it just appears intelligent. To really develop intelligence, it would have to interact actively with its environment and move within it (Fig. 1).

The next perspective explained by Lawrence Shapiro in the year 2011 is the replacement perspective. The replacement perspective says, in general terms, that the classic understanding of cognition should be replaced with a definition in which the brain has an important function but is downgraded "from a star to a co-star, an equal partner in the creation of cognition alongside body and world" as Shapiro put it [10]. Proponents of the replacement perspective emphasize the situatedness of cognition. Situatedness of cognition means that the properties of the world (e.g., sunlight) determine what

Fig. 1 The Chinese room. *(Based on an idea of Searle, 1980, Figure drawn by Farina Klein.)*

possibilities a person has relative to their body. The properties of the environment thus also determine what information and possibilities the individual has. The term "sunlight" can be used as an example to explain this. The sunlight in the world allows us to see, influences our sleep-wake rhythm, and much more. If the properties of sunlight change, we change too—our bodies, our perceptions, and our cognitive processes.

Rodney Brooks from MIT in the United States in 1991 was the first one to apply the replacement perspective to robotics. The trigger was the robot "Shakey," developed and based on the "sense-model-plan-act" structure: Shakey had a camera in front as a sensor (sense). A computer used the input from the camera to construct a symbolic model, which in turn was used by a program (STRIPS) to give the robot a command to move in a certain direction (plan) based on the description of the environment, which the robot then executed (act). Shakey's task was, among other things, to navigate through a simple space and avoid objects standing around. Shakey was very slow and very bad at this task because creating a new model was very time consuming and inefficient. Shakey shows how a robot is built from a classic cognitive theory perspective: The most important steps, the steps that determine the robot's behavior, take place in a computer outside the actual robot body. The "brain" of the robot is thus literally disembodied.

In his attempt to improve the robots existing at the time, Rodney Brooks was inspired by the embodied cognition idea of situatedness. He then constructed the robot "Allen," which was based on a completely different system from Shakey's. Instead of building on the classic sense-model-plan-act structure, he linked perception directly to the robot's action. This new robot was much faster and more efficiently able to perform its task (walking through a room without hitting anything).

The embodied cognition perspective fueled a groundbreaking first step toward increasingly independent moving robots. This can be seen, for example, at the annual Robot Soccer World Cup (RoboCup). There, two robot teams play against each other for the title. The officially formulated goal of the RoboCup is that by 2050 at the latest, the winning team of the RoboCup will win against the best human, professional soccer team at that time as published by Kitano and Asada in 1998 [11]. Even if this ambitious goal is considered unlikely from a sport psychological perspective as I wrote elsewhere [12], the soccer skills of robots are improving at a rapid pace. In fact, the RoboCup 2016 was the first time that a robot team won a soccer match against a human soccer team—even if not against a professional one (https://www.youtube.com/watch?v=9CNuTSxVwt4).

The last perspective explained by Shapiro is the constitution perspective. This perspective claims, in general terms, that cognition basically includes the body (and the environment), rather than cognition being influenced by one's own body and environment. In other words, the body, its movement, and its environment are cognition. Consequently, supporters of the constitution perspective often argue that the term cognition needs to be replaced with a broader definition that includes the body, its movements, and the environment. Influential proponents of the constitution hypothesis include Andy Clark [13], Kevin O'Regan and Alva Noë [14], and Robert Wilson [15].

A theory particularly relevant to embodied cognition is the sensorimotor theory of perceptual experience developed by Kevin O'Regan and Alva Noë. This theory is based on the view that we perceive the world as we do because we learn sensorimotor contingencies between our movements and the resulting perceived changes in the environment. According to the theory, a ball looks like a ball because it looks like this as soon as we move our eyes.

All three embodied cognition approaches presented here and discussed in length by Lawrence Shapiro make it clear that the body, its movements, and its environment should be included in the study of mental processes to get valid conclusions. This applies bidirectionally: When investigating the body and its movements, mental processes and environmental conditions should be considered as I will illustrate in Chapter 4 in more detail.

How can we describe how movements shape cognition? Consider, for example, the well-known phrase, "Mens sana in corpore sano" (a healthy mind in a healthy body). Recent metaanalyses [16] have shown that this saying of the Roman poet Juvenal, meant to be ironic almost 2000 years ago, contains at least a bit of truth. Developmental psychology studies have shown that especially children [17] and older people [18] benefit from regular exercise. These general, long-term influences of movement on cognition do not directly speak to embodied cognition research and are therefore not discussed in more detail. Embodied cognition research is mainly concerned with very specific, rather short-term effects of exercise on cognition. Therefore in the following, we report studies that investigated whether certain movements influence cognitive processes and if so, how. For example, later we will discuss how movements such as an upright posture (as in horse show jumping) or downward bent (as in hockey) change memory processes? Is there any benefit in taking a so-called power pose before a competition to begin the competition with confidence?

What do you think of when you see someone walking upright? Probably concepts such as good mood, pride, joy, and self-confidence come to mind. On the other hand, what do you think of when you see someone walking bent over? Probably concepts such as bad mood, humility, sadness, and low self-esteem are more likely. So, it seems that certain concepts are automatically associated with certain gait patterns. In a study by Johannes Michalak and colleagues from the University of Bochum [19] in 2015, it was experimentally examined whether positive (or negative) concepts are activated by an upright (or bent) gait. The starting point was the fact that several studies have shown a close connection between a flexed gait and depression [20]. In a preliminary study, the researchers compared the movements of a group of depression patients in a depressive phase with a group of healthy people. They found that the depressed people walked more slowly, swung their arms less, moved their upper extremities vertically to a lesser extent, swayed more to the left and right with their bodies, and took a more bent and forward-leaning position than healthy people (Michalak et al. [21]; for a demonstration of happy and depressed walking styles, see https://www.biomotionlab.ca/html5-bml-walker/). Johannes Michalak's lab then manipulated people's gait by letting them walk on a treadmill and giving them online feedback on their gait patterns. A display mounted in front of the participants was programmed so that the bar on the display deflected to the right for one-half of the participants when they walked upright and to the right for the other half when they walked bent. The participants were instructed to walk in such a way that the bar in front of them moved to the right. The authors hypothesized that a bent and depressed gait would activate more negatively associated words and an upright and happy gait would activate more positively associated words. This was measured with a memory task: The participants were given 20 words (10 positive, 10 negative) to read before the movement manipulation. After the movement manipulation they were asked to name as many words as possible. Indeed, the participants who walked bent during the movement manipulation remembered more negative words than positive words compared with the participants who walked upright. Activation of a concept by performing movements associated with this concept is not limited to positive and negative words. Thomas Mussweiler now at the London Business School, United Kingdom showed in 2006 [22] that a sluggish gait activates the concept "overweight" and a very slow gait activates the concept "elderly" (but see a current debate on the difficulty of replication of priming studies [23]).

What are the mechanisms by which the activation of certain concepts is realized during execution of movement patterns? One possible process is neurophysiological reenactment as introduced by Lawrence Barsalou in 1999 [9]. This means that information (e.g., the concept "depression") consists of neuronal activation patterns that include, among other things, certain movements or perceptions. This information is stored by neurons in adjacent associative fields as assumed by Antonio Damasio and Hanna Damasio [24]. If a certain movement is now carried out, this results in a partial reactivation of the entire concept (e.g., the concept "depression").

Under what circumstances does the mechanism described have an influence on our behavior? Do we perform better if we adopt a so-called power pose before a competition to activate the concept of "self-confidence" and accordingly enter the competition with confidence? For some time now, the media (including *The New York Times* [25]) have been propagating the idea that power poses have an influence on various behavioral and hormonal parameters. A high-power pose is a pose that takes up a lot of space, is directed upward, and radiates overall strength and self-confidence. In contrast, a low-power pose is a pose that takes up little space, is directed downward, and overall tends to radiate weakness and low self-confidence.

The evidence regarding the effect of power posing is mixed: On the one hand, studies have reported that a high-power pose produces an increased self-reported feeling of strength compared with a low-power pose as shown by Amy Cuddy [26]. In addition, physiological responses have been measured such as cortisol. High-power poses lead to a lower cortisol level and an increased testosterone level [27]. Further, high-power poses improve self-esteem and motivation [28]. Amy Cuddy and colleagues showed improved performance in a job interview as well [26]. On a more negative side, high-power posing is not good for all situations. For example, high-power poses have been shown to increases risk behavior [29] and cognitive bias (e.g., the tendency to remember negative rather than positive words) in depressed people [30]. On the other hand, studies have reported that high-power poses do not increase risk behavior compared with low-power poses [31]. The positive effects on the physiological level such as hormone transmitters has been recently not replicated and for instances its unclear whether indeed high-power poses increase testosterone levels [32]. On a psychological level some studies find no increased self-reported feeling of strength [31] and thus it may be premature to say which findings are reliable enough to conclude. Differences in the study results show that the activation of a particular concept by a particular movement does not happen at any time and under any circumstances but rather is probably modulated by many factors, such as social [33] or developmental factors [34]. Accordingly, a challenge for embodied cognition research is to identify these modulating factors and to test them in ecologically valid settings, such as sport settings.

Here is an example from a national team soccer player in Germany:

> *I'm an interpreter of space. Every good, successful player, especially an attacking player, has a well-developed sense of space and time. It's not a phenomenon you only find in two or three people on earth. Every great striker knows it's all about the timing between the person who plays the pass and the person making a run into the right zone.*

Thomas Müller, former German National Team player and Bayern Munich player [35]

This quote by Thomas Müller impressively shows the importance of temporal and spatial concepts in sport. As explained in the section on the theoretical framework of embodied cognition approaches, one of the assumptions of the embodied cognition perspective is that our ability to form and understand concepts is based on the fact that (and how) we move with our body in the world. Thus concepts are created by combining bits of information from perception, movement, and mental states and connecting them in a meaningful way. Take the spatial concept "in front," for example: We can *perceive*, say, where a dog has its front. We can *move* forward. And we can *imagine* a ball being shot forward. All this information is combined to form the overall concept "in front." If we now take the temporal concept "future," things become more complicated: We cannot *perceive* the future. We cannot *move* into the future (except with a time machine, of course). But we can still *imagine* the future. So, time has no direct relation to the body, but we still have a concept of time. Are abstract concepts (such as time), which are not directly perceptible through sensorimotor experience, a contradiction to the embodied cognition assumption that concepts are multimodal, created by the sensorimotor experiences of our body? Not necessarily: Remember the earlier argument by George Lakoff and Mark Johnson that states that abstract concepts are built on more concrete concepts. For time and space, this means that abstract, temporal concepts are built on concrete, spatial concepts. As briefly explained in this chapter's Introduction, this is reflected in the fact that temporal relationships are often represented by spatial expressions. "My 20th birthday is approaching" or "We are moving toward summer" are examples. In both sentences a spatial expression (something is approaching, moving toward something) is used to represent a temporal relationship. Looking at the content of these two sentences, it is noticeable that time is represented by two different frames of reference [36]. In the first sentence, the person is stationary and time approaches (time-moving reference frame), while in the second sentence people are actively moving through time (ego-moving reference frame). Through ambiguous, temporal questions, it is now possible to find out what kind of time-moving reference frame someone has.

How would you spontaneously answer the following question: "The soccer training is usually every day at 3:30 pm. Tomorrow's training has been moved forward 1 hour. What time is the training now that it has been rescheduled?" If your answer is "2:30 pm" you are among the 50% of people who answer in a time-moving frame of reference. If your answer is "4:30 pm" you are among the 50% of people who answer in an ego-moving frame of reference.

Similarly, one can find out what spatial frame of reference someone has by asking ambiguous, spatial questions. When Lera Boroditsky from Stanford University asked participants such questions, the answer distribution in English-speaking samples was usually 50/50.

How would you spontaneously answer the following question: "The golf instructor asks Max to putt into the front hole. What color is the hole that Max is supposed to putt into?" If your answer is "red" you are among the 50% of people who answer in a time-moving frame of reference. If your answer is "blue" you are among the 50% of people who answer in an ego-moving frame of reference (Fig. 2).

Whether and under what conditions one or the other frame of reference is preferred depends among other things on cultural norms and language as

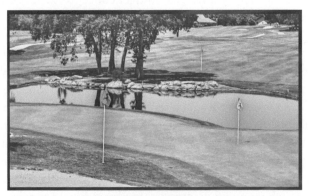

Fig. 2 The golf instructor asks Max to putt into the front hole. What color is the hole that Max is supposed to putt into? *(Figure drawn by Max Roebel.)*

Lera Boroditsky argued [37]. Several studies have shown that the spatial frame of reference influences the temporal frame, but that the temporal frame of reference does not influence the spatial frame to the same extent [38]. This observation supports George Lakoff and Mark Johnson's assumption that more abstract temporal concepts are based on more concrete spatial concepts and suggests a fundamental space-time asymmetry. Is this asymmetry really a fundamental phenomenon, or does it arise from pieces of information of varying degrees of precision that are represented? One way to find out is to represent the temporal dimension more clearly and distinctly than the spatial dimension. For example, Zhenguang Cai and Louise Connell [39] from the University of Manchester, United Kingdom, asked participants to touch physical sticks while listening to an auditory note and then reproduce either the length of the stick or the duration of the note. In three experiments, participants could either only feel the physical stick or they could feel and see the stick. Results indicate that when spatial information relies on touch, the effect of time on space is substantially stronger than the effect of space on time. This effect was not found when participants could also see the stick. This indicates that the space-time asymmetry is not a fundamental phenomenon but rather depends on the mode of representation and the associated information content a recent overview of studies indicated [40].

The connection between movement and the associated access to temporal and spatial information is particularly important in the context of sports, when temporal information is transformed into spatial information, as in dance, for example: Music carries mainly temporal information (e.g., rhythm), which is translated into spatial information by the dancer. A new technological development also makes the other direction possible: Body movements are translated into music in real time (software "Nagual Dance" http://www.nagualsounds.com/about-us/technology/). Thus no temporal (acoustic) information is transformed into spatial information, but spatial information is transformed into temporal (acoustic) information. This opens new movement horizons and changes the existing transformation flow.

In summary, the interactions between movement, time, and space play an important role in many applications as well—be it in instructions (Please stand in front of the bars in a physical education class), in the physiological and psychological effects of upright or bent postures, or in dance, where temporal information is translated into spatial information (or vice versa) through movement. This chapter informs about the concept of embodied cognition and how our bodies and movements shape our thinking. Given that movements are our observable interaction with the environment, it is important to consider how the combination of both the body and the environment affect our thinking.

References

[1] This chapter is based on a chapter on Embodied cognition fromJ. Loeffler, R. Cañal-Bruland, M. Raab, Embodied cognition, in: J. Schüler, M. Wegner, H. Plessner (Eds.), Lehrbuch Sportpsychologie—Theoretische Grundlagen und Anwendungen, Textbook of Sportpsychology—Theoretical Foundations and Applications Springer-Verlag, Berlin, Heidelberg, 2020, pp. 115–140.
[2] See https://en.wikipedia.org/wiki/Embodied_cognition.
[3] E. Thelen, G. Schöner, C. Scheier, L.B. Smith, The dynamics of embodiment: a field theory of infant perseverative reaching, Behav. Brain Sci. 24 (1) (2001) 1-34-86. Definition is from page 1.
[4] M. Rowlands, The New Science of the Mind: From Extended Mind to Embodied Phenomenology, MIT Press, Cambridge, MA, 2010.
[5] For a virtual reality study, seeP.W. Fink, P.S. Foo, W.H. Warren, Catching fly balls in virtual reality: a critical test of the outfielder problem. J. Vis. 9 (13) (2009) 14, https://doi.org/10.1167/9.13.14; For a seminal paper on catching fly balls, seeM.K. McBeath, D.M. Shaffer, M.K. Kaiser, How baseball outfielders determine where to run to catch fly balls, Science (New York, N.Y.) 268 (5210) (1995) 569–573; For a study of strategies used by dogs to catch flying objects, seeD.M. Shaffer, S.M. Krauchunas, M. Eddy, M.K. McBeath, How dogs navigate to catch frisbees. Psychol. Sci. 15 (7) (2004) 437–441, https://doi.org/10.1111/j.0956-7976.2004.00698.x.
[6] M. Merleau-Ponty, Phenomenology of Perception, Routledge, London, UK, 2002 Cite is from p. 525.
[7] L. Shapiro, Embodied Cognition, Routledge Press, New York, 2011.
[8] G. Lakoff, M. Johnson, Philosophy in the Flesh: The Embodied Mind and Its Challenge to Western Thought, Basic Books, New York, NY, 1999 Cite is from p. 34.
[9] L.W. See Barsalou, Perceptual symbol systems, Behav. Brain Sci. 22 (4) (1999) 577–660.
[10] L. Shapiro, Embodied Cognition, Routledge Press, New York, 2011 Cite is from p. 137.
[11] H. Kitano, M. Asada, RoboCup humanoid challenge: that's one small step for a robot, one giant leap for mankind. in: Proceedings 1998 IEEE/RSJ International Conference on Intelligent Robots and Systems. Innovations in Theory, Practice and Applications (Cat. No. 98CH36190), vol. 1, 1998, pp. 419–424, https://doi.org/10.1109/IROS.1998.724655.
[12] M. Raab, Sport and exercise psychology 2050. Ger. J. Sport Sci. (2017). https://doi.org/10.1007/s12662-016-0435-y.
[13] A. Clark, Supersizing the Mind: Embodiment, Action, and Cognitive Extension, Oxford University Press, USA, 2008.
[14] J.K. O'Regan, A. Noë, A sensorimotor account of vision and visual consciousness, Behav. Brain Sci. 24 (5) (2001) 939-973-1031.
[15] R.A. Wilson, Boundaries of the Mind: The Individual in the Fragile Sciences—Cognition, Cambridge University Press, Cambridge, UK, 2004.
[16] See meta-analyses of, L.G. Johnson, M.L. Butson, R.C. Polman, I.S. Raj, E. Borkoles, D. Scott, … G. Jones, Light physical activity is positively associated with cognitive performance in older community dwelling adults. J. Sci. Med. Sport 19 (11) (2016) 877–882, https://doi.org/10.1016/j.jsams.2016.02.002; G. Kennedy, R.J. Hardman, H. Macpherson, A.B. Scholey, A. Pipingas, How does exercise reduce

the rate of age-associated cognitive decline? A review of potential mechanisms. J. Alzheimers Dis. 55 (1) (2017) 1–18, https://doi.org/10.3233/JAD-160665.

[17] M.H. Bornstein, C.-S. Hahn, J.T.D. Suwalsky, Physically developed and exploratory young infants contribute to their own long-term academic achievement. Psychol. Sci. 24 (10) (2013) 1906–1917, https://doi.org/10.1177/09567976 13479974.

[18] E. Scherder, R. Scherder, L. Verburgh, M. Königs, M. Blom, A.F. Kramer, L. Eggermont, Executive functions of sedentary elderly may benefit from walking: a systematic review and meta-analysis. Am. J. Geriatr. Psychiatry 22 (8) (2014) 782–791, https://doi.org/10.1016/j.jagp.2012.12.026.

[19] J. Michalak, K. Rohde, N.F. Troje, How we walk affects what we remember: gait modifications through biofeedback change negative affective memory bias. J. Behav. Ther. Exp. Psychiatry 46 (2015) 121–125, https://doi.org/10.1016/j.jbtep.2014.09.004.

[20] See for instance M.R. Lemke, T. Wendorff, B. Mieth, K. Buhl, M. Linnemann, Spatiotemporal gait patterns during over ground locomotion in major depression compared with healthy controls. J. Psychiatr. Res. 34 (4–5) (2000) 277–283, https://doi.org/10.1016/S0022-3956(00)00017-0.

[21] J. Michalak, N.F. Troje, J. Fischer, P. Vollmar, T. Heidenreich, D. Schulte, Embodiment of sadness and depression—gait patterns associated with dysphoric mood. Psychosom. Med. 71 (5) (2009) 580–587, https://doi.org/10.1097/PSY.0b013e3181a2515c.

[22] T. Mussweiler, Doing is for thinking!: stereotype activation by stereotypic movements, Psychol. Sci. 17 (1) (2006) 17–21.

[23] See issues on replicating these finding S. Doyen, O. Klein, C.-L. Pichon, A. Cleeremans, Behavioral priming: it's all in the mind, but whose mind?. PLoS One 7 (1) (2012) e29081, https://doi.org/10.1371/journal.pone.0029081.

[24] A.R. Damasio, H. Damasio, Cortical systems for retrieval of concrete knowledge: the convergence zone framework, in: C. Koch, J.L. Davis (Eds.), Large-Scale Neuronal Theories of the Brain, MIT Press, Cambridge, MA, 1994, pp. 61–74.

[25] D. Hochman, Amy Cuddy takes a stand, N.Y. Times (2014) September 19. Retrieved from: https://www.nytimes.com/2014/09/21/fashion/amy-cuddy-takes-a-stand-TED-talk.html.

[26] J. Cuddy, C.A. Wilmuth, A.J. Yap, D.R. Carney, Preparatory power posing affects nonverbal presence and job interview performance. J. Appl. Psychol. 100 (4) (2015) 1286–1295, https://doi.org/10.1037/a0038543.

[27] D.R. Carney, A.J.C. Cuddy, A.J. Yap, Power posing: brief nonverbal displays affect neuroendocrine levels and risk tolerance. Psychol. Sci. 21 (10) (2010) 1363–1368, https://doi.org/10.1177/0956797610383437.

[28] J. Fischer, P. Fischer, B. Englich, N. Aydin, D. Frey, Empower my decisions: the effects of power gestures on confirmatory information processing. J. Exp. Soc. Psychol. 47 (6) (2011) 1146–1154, https://doi.org/10.1016/j.jesp.2011.06.008.

[29] L. Huang, A.D. Galinsky, D.H. Gruenfeld, L.E. Guillory, Powerful postures versus powerful roles—which is the proximate correlate of thought and behavior?. Psychol. Sci. 22 (1) (2011) 95–102, https://doi.org/10.1177/0956797610391912.

[30] J. Michalak, J. Mischnat, T. Teismann, Sitting posture makes a difference-embodiment effects on depressive memory bias. Clin. Psychol. Psychother. 21 (6) (2014) 519–524, https://doi.org/10.1002/cpp.1890.

[31] K.E. Garrison, D. Tang, B.J. Schmeichel, Embodying power: a preregistered replication and extension of the power pose effect. Soc. Psychol. Personal. Sci. 7 (7) (2016) 623–630, https://doi.org/10.1177/1948550616652209.

[32] R. Ronay, J.M. Tybur, D. van Huijstee, M. Morssinkhof, Embodied power, testosterone, and overconfidence as a causal pathway to risk-taking. Compr. Results Soc. Psychol. vol. 2, (1) (2016) 28–43, https://doi.org/10.1080/23743603.2016.1248081.

[33] E. Ranehill, A. Dreber, M. Johannesson, S. Leiberg, S. Sul, R.A. Weber, Assessing the robustness of power posing: no effect on hormones and risk tolerance in a large sample of men and women, Psychol. Sci. 26 (5) (2015) 653–656.

[34] J. Löffler, M. Raab, R. Cañal-Bruland, A lifespan perspective on embodied cognition. Front. Psychol. (2016), https://doi.org/10.3389/fpsyg.2016.00845.

[35] U. Hesse, Thomas Müller: the modest assassin, The Guardian (2016) February 23. Retrieved from: https://www.theguardian.com/football/2016/feb/23/thomas-muller-modest-assassin-bayern-munich-germany.

[36] L. Boroditsky, Metaphoric structuring: understanding time through spatial metaphors. Cognition 75 (1) (2000) 1–28, https://doi.org/10.3389/fpsyg.2013.00142.

[37] L. Boroditsky, Does language shape thought? Mandarin and English speakers' conceptions of time. Cogn. Psychol. 43 (1) (2001) 1–22, https://doi.org/10.1006/cogp.2001.0748.

[38] D. Casasanto, L. Boroditsky, Time in the mind: using space to think about time. Cognition 106 (2) (2008) 579–593, https://doi.org/10.1016/j.cognition.2007.03.004.

[39] Z.G. Cai, L. Connell, Space-time interdependence: evidence against asymmetric mapping between time and space. Cognition 136 (2015) 268–281, https://doi.org/10.1016/j.cognition.2014.11.039.

[40] J. Löffler, R. Cañal-Bruland, A. Schröger, J.W. Tolentino-Castro, M. Raab, Interrelations between temporal and spatial cognition: the role of modality-specific processing. Front. Psychol. 9 (2018) 2609, https://doi.org/10.3389/fpsyg.2018.02609.

CHAPTER FOUR

How the body and the environment affect our thinking?

I wrote this chapter during a sabbatical period in Israel at the Wingate College in Netanya. The hotel was about 10 min from the beach, and every morning and every evening, I tried to take a long walk on the beach. To go down to the beach, you have two options: take approximately thousand stairs and a long detour or take the elevator right to the beach. Well, I took the stairs, the first few days. But my preference changed when I was hungry after some long walks, my feet got sunburned, or when it was getting dark. I have read about the studies by Dennis R. Proffitt (University of Virginia, United States) and others showing that the perception of the slant of a hill—or in my case, the slant upward of the stairs—increases if the perceiver is more fatigued, wearing a heavy backpack, or experiencing low blood sugar [1]. In these experiments, participants need not even climb up the hill, they were asked to judge. Why did body conditions influence these judgments? It seems that the university students who participated in these experiments likely anticipated walking uphill and implicitly considered the weight of the backpack they were carrying or the current status of their body. Although there have been criticism and alternative interpretations of these results [2], it seems that the body at least has its say in such tasks.

I remember my trip to New Zealand in which I went climbing by myself. Did my choice of a specific route's length and difficulty change depending on whether I made my decision before or after breakfast? If Proffitt and colleagues are correct, I would have chosen a more difficult and a longer trip after breakfast. Did making this decision in the mountains with a hot cup of sugared coffee in my hand and warm clothes on my back increase my overconfidence, leading me to make a potentially harmful decision? Clearly, I survived, even if, as for many decisions, the current status of my body played a silent, guiding role. Sometimes the body can lead more than the cognitive system; we with our self-serving bias might think we have a free will [3], but do we really?

What about gesturing? Depending on our culture and personal preferences, we do this to different degrees, but it has been shown that gesturing when solving math problems is quite beneficial: Gesturers did better than a group of participants who were told to sit on their hands [4]. We also gesture when it clearly serves no communicative purpose, such as when talking on the telephone. Is talking and gesturing simply a motor program that produces activations not only of our vocal motor system but also of our arms and hands? Many studies suggest that gesturing is not just an outflow of the motor system but actually can help people understand or solve problems. Similarly, people solving math problems with water in their mouth did not do as well as a comparable group that could mouth their way through the calculations and equations.

Handedness also plays a role. I am left-handed, and being in this minority has not bothered me too much. In sports being a left-hander can actually be advantageous, and it has been shown that for sports in which it matters, such as tennis and fencing, there are more left-handers (about 20% or more) than you would expect from the population, which is about 10% left-handed worldwide. However, left and right in gesturing seem to matter to our conversational partners. For example, gestures with the right hand have been found to convey positive information and gestures with the left, negative information when performed by a right-hander [5]. Interestingly, your arguments may resonate or the impression you make may be more lasting depending on whether you gesture with the preferred hand of the observer; given that most people are right-handed, in my case, this may not be my preferred hand. Are my talks simply perceived as less compelling and my first impression less exciting by right-handers? I hope not, given the alternative explanations that come easily to my mind.

Not only gestures but also hand movements in general do influence our thinking. Specifically the hands and fingers seem to be important for numerical cognition. For example, children who have good finger dexterity are also good at simple numerical calculations [6]. Likewise, it has been reported that playing an instrument such as the piano trains hands and fingers and allows better processing of cognitive tasks in which fingers are useful tools for adding or subtracting. It therefore makes sense to prepare your presentations with gestures that enhance memory and produce support for your arguments, such as pointing up to emphasize a great idea. Using the words up and down in an experiment is one way to prime movements that influence your thinking. Another way to influence your thinking is to produce up or downward movements when solving a task. Here is an example. Daniel Casasanto [7], now at Cornell University, did a study in which participants were asked to move marbles from a middle shelf to either an upper shelf or a lower shelf while generating memories of events from their past. As up is associated with positive things and emotions and down with more negative things and emotions, people generally generated more positive memories in the group that lifted marbles up and vice versa, more negative memories in the group shifting the marbles down a shelf. This effect has been found not only for a person's own movements but also when observing people making up or down movements or actually moving an object up or down. For example, Janna Gottwald of Uppsala University in Sweden and colleagues asked participants in three experiments to rate emotionally neutral objects, such as a coffee mug, regarding its likelihood as a gift, or their willingness to pay. Gift likelihood and willingness to pay ratings are assumed to be an indication of the objects' valence, that is, how much the participants' like or dislike the object. Participants in the studies saw videos of other people who displayed moving an object to either a higher or a lower position from a middle position. Participants rated objects more positively, that is, they were willing to pay more or considered the object more likely to be a gift, when the object was moved up compared with when it was moved down (Fig. 1) [8].

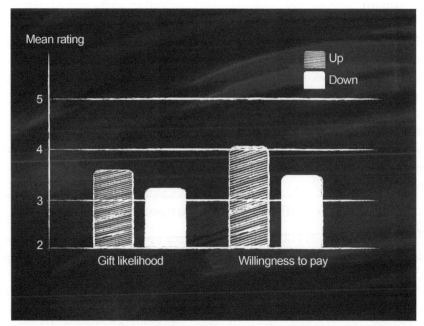

Fig. 1 Ratings of gift likelihood and willingness to pay, depending on whether the object was moved to an upper or lower position on the shelves.

Here is another example of how left and right movements are related to our thinking. In school, we are trained with a mental number line with increasing numbers from left to right. When students are asked to produce movements and simultaneously randomly generate numbers, they often generate small numbers with movements to the left and large numbers if the movements are to the right [9].

Another interesting finding is that movements even influence abstract concepts such as representations of time and space that you cannot experience, as the earlier-mentioned example demonstrated with the math number line. If I said to you, "Next week's Wednesday meeting is moved forward by two days," when will the meeting take place, Monday or Friday? In a number of studies this question was ambiguous: 50% answered Monday and the other half Friday. However, when participants walked backward, the likelihood of answering Monday increased [10]. In our lab, Jonna Löffler did a PhD just on evaluating whether it matters if you move in space or just walk forward/backward on a treadmill (it does not matter), whether you test backward-walking athletes (they even have a world championship) or us regular folk (it matters), and whether you ask the question in London or Cologne, given the language-specific difference between Brits and Germans (it matters).

Finally, just as up is associated with positive things and emotions, and down with more negative things and emotions, thoughts about one's past and future can also be influenced by movement. For example, standing in line is a boring task that takes time. Whether you are standing at the end of the line or close to the head of the line, it matters in answering a question about the future or past [11]. When traveling in Germany, I often take the fast and convenient trains. Considering all the earlier-mentioned researches, would it be better for my thinking if I sit facing forward when thinking about my future plans and maybe face backward when thinking about my past?

Movements influence our emotional judgments

A famous study [12] showed that putting a pen between the teeth caused people to rate cartoons as funnier than when they held the pen between their lips (Fig. 2). Why is that so?

Movements are often related to a person's emotional state, such as walking slump-shouldered when depressed or upright when in a happy mood. Likewise, movements can modulate emotions. This is why depressed patients have exercise programs to increase dopamine production, which is related

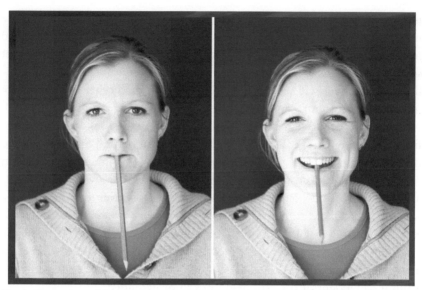

Fig. 2 Illustration of the two ways in which participants were instructed to position the pen for rating the funniness of cartoons. Left panel: the pen is held with the teeth, inducing a facial expression similar to smiling. Right panel: the pen is held with the lips, inducing a facial expression similar to pouting. *(Available at: http://tinyurl.com/zm7p917 under CC license https://creativecommons.org/licenses/by/2.0/.)*

to emotional rise. Further, smiling or laughing therapies have been advocated and empirically validated. When you put a pen between your teeth, your face with over 40 muscles will activate those that are related to smiling. The smiling activation signals your limbic system, responsible for emotional regulation in the brain and indicates that you are in a positive mood, which makes you find cartoons funnier. If you have the pen between your lips, the smile muscles are not activated and thus you find the cartoon less funny. Recently a lab could not replicate this finding [13]. It seems that these effects happen under specific conditions [14] in which people do not feel monitored or are not monitoring themselves.

Facial muscles are not the only one having an emotional effect on your judgments. An overview of the effects of moving eyes, arms, legs, and the whole body showed nicely how much is currently known [15]. For example, bending the arm to yourself is associated with something good, such as bringing a liked food to your mouth, whereas pushing something away is often associated with avoiding bad things. It has been shown that indeed, arm flexions result in positive and creative thinking and arm extensions in the opposite, that is, less creative thinking [16]. A colleague and I extended findings of this kind by showing that the intention of the movement is more important than the body's position, as the movement effects are represented in the movement goals. You might pull a trigger (flexion) to achieve that some is moving away from you such as a bullet. If you watch animals or children playing, you will see that they actually push each other away with the intention of prompting approach and continuing the play. In our study [17], we separated the movement direction (flexion vs extension) of the right arm from the movement goal (push something away or toward oneself). We did this by building a push–pull lever and asking students in an extended-arm condition and a flexed-arm condition to move it either away from (avoidance goal) or toward (approach goal) themselves. During the movements, students were asked to generate words about a given target word, such as tree. We found that if people had an approach goal (independent of the arm being flexed or extended), they generated more positive words that are associated with trees than those students who had an avoidance goal, again independent of the arm being flexed or extended.

A group of researchers took the exact opposite approach, asking whether providing words and increasing perceptual fluency would produce more approach movements. Carr, Rotteveel, and Winkielman asked participants for their gut reaction to the presented pseudowords (things that sound like real words but have no meaning) as to whether they liked or disliked these words or whether these words could be categorized as a living or a nonliving item. The first task was meant to produce affective judgments in which approach and avoidance movements are related to word processing. In the nonaffective living-versus-nonliving categorization judgments, the effects should not be present. Responses were made by pressing a button on a vertical stand: either a top button that was further away and reached with an extended arm if they did not like a pseudoword or a closer bottom button reached with an arm flexion movement if they liked a word. The words presented were either easy or hard to read, and it was predicted that the easy-to-read words would produce perceptual fluency that would activate faster approach movements—that is participants would press the bottom button near the body faster for easy-to-read than for hard-to-read words. This finding was most pronounced when the task was actually to produce affective judgments, such as like/dislike, and less when judging nonaffective categorizations such as living/nonliving. Importantly the fluent easy-to-read pseudowords produced responses of the smiling muscles, measured by electromyography [18], indicating further support of the smiling study effect.

How do gut feelings lead to embodied choices?

If you are in love, why do you have butterflies in your stomach? If you are stressed, why do you have a stomachache? These connections, often referred to as the brain-gut axis, show that the brain influences the status of your gut. Recently, researchers have tested whether the association works the other way around, that is, if our gut feelings are actually the cause of some of the thinking and feeling we subjectively experience. How might that work? Multiple pathways run for instance from the hypothalamus to the gastrointestinal microbiota and from the brain via the vagus nerve to the gastrointestinal lumen. In the laboratory, stressing people is often done by requiring them to perform highly demanding tests under expert observation. Participants often self-report being stressed, but researchers also use the objective measure of cortisol, the so-called stress hormone, which is produced when someone is stressed. Cortisol is well known to have an effect on the gastrointestinal microbiota, so researchers are able to test whether the implementation of stress causes changes in the gut that can be measured by direct changes in gut behavior, and long-term effects can be assessed using the stool of participants to see whether there are changes in the microbiota when a person is stressed for longer times.

Gut feelings such as first impressions about people, your intuitive decisions about what food to eat, or risking a gamble are actually products of your "second brain" [19] the gut. In the social sciences, gut feelings refer to human affective states and intuitive choices that are often defined as unconscious choices that are detached from logic. Consider again, for example, Charles Darwin's notes on the pros and cons of marrying. Although the list of cons and his analysis led to the conclusion that marriage was not advisable, Darwin's intuition clearly differed from this conclusion, as evidenced by his final decision to marry and to close the note with QED as a completion of the proof of irrationality.

The study by Shai Danzinger (Ben Gurion University of the Negev, Israel) and colleagues [20] that I mentioned earlier drew me into the area of intuition even more. I will describe it in a bit more detail here, as it had a big impact on me. The study showed that judges' decisions in court differed depending on whether the judges were hungry or satiated. The analyses revealed that favorable rulings dropped from 65% to near zero from the early mornings to just before lunch and rose again to 65% after lunch. Assuming that the accused and the specific cases are randomly ordered or at least not ordered on their severity, the data really made me wonder about my own behavior. I call Fridays my judgment day, as I make most of my professional decisions on that day, such as evaluating student exams, reviewing scientific papers for publication in journals for which I have been a reviewer or editor, and assessing grant applications, as well as making promotion and hiring recommendations within my own and other universities. Some of these tasks are completed before lunch, and some after lunch. After reading the study, I asked myself whether I had maybe been too strict or too lenient in my judgments depending on my hunger level, without consciously reflecting on it at the time. Such choices have important consequences. Did some people thus get lucky and others suffer just because I worked on their case before or after my spaghetti Bolognese? I can tell you, I was quite happy to read the paper [21] by my colleague Andreas Glöckner (University of Hagen, Germany) in which he argued that the effect of "hungry judges" may be overestimated, but still my gut was not fully convinced. I went looking for more information, and here I share some of what I have learned over the last few years.

In the past century, research on intuition (from the Latin *intueor* to consider, or look at, immediate cognition) has described many different processes, encompassing different disciplines and constructs, that relate choices to behavior, for example, perception, cognition, and affect [22]. However, those processes have previously been studied in isolation, and discussions of theory have often been simplified by separating intuitive from deliberative choices [23]. Such research strategies have recently been labeled as dual-process accounts, and they are nowadays deemed insufficient [24] to describe choice behavior. From my own research, I am now better able to understand interactions between cognitive and affective choices, now that I have studied fast choices based on simple intuitive heuristics from a neuroscience perspective [25], computationally modeled how early fixations of gaze predict later choices [26], and developed methodological paradigms that test cognitive and affective choices on a behavioral level [27]. The latter work was cited by Nobel laureate Daniel Kahneman, who emphasized that such process can be tested in natural environments [28]. Recent progress in theory development has led to a theoretical account of embodied choices [29] and a decision-making model [30] that formally describes how these choices are learned. I will provide you with some of this background later but in a nutshell, these intuitive choices make up a large percentage of the decisions we make in our lives and can be explained by embodied choices.

Embodied choice models assume that the sensorimotor system itself provides cues for choices. Sensorimotor cues have been ignored in research, whereas cues referring to cost-benefit analyses or the cognitive examination of complex calculations of expected values are overrepresented in choice research. For embodied choices, the execution of an action is thus not just the end product of a cognitive choice between two options, but a cue indicating whether one or the other option is advantageous. Further, it seems likely that information from interoception and exteroception run in parallel and are based on experience [31]. Such arguments have been tested on simple behavior and recently the concept has been extended and revised for movement performance.

For embodied choices, people must have expertise about their own body as well as skill expertise; their body awareness drives gut feelings. In recent studies, you often see researchers evaluate interoception as a moderator of choices, and it indeed may change the way we choose and trust our instincts. Barney D. Dunn (Medical Research Council Cognition and Brain Science Unit, Cambridge, England), for example, found that the quality of a person's interoception measured by heartbeat perception modulated the strength of the relationship between bodily reactions and cognitive-affective processing in an adaptive intuitive decision-making task called the intuitive reasoning task [32]. This task is based on the Iowa gambling task, a frequently used task in decision-making research. With the goal of earning as much money as possible, participants choose a card from one of four virtual card decks to predict whether the next card drawn from one of the decks will have the same or a different color from a card in front of them (Fig. 3). Unbeknownst to the participants, some decks have a low probability and others a higher probability of producing a win.

It seems that participants' bodily reactions inform them about the "good" and "bad" decks, but this is moderated by how well they can interoceptively use bodily information. Of course, interoception can be damaged, as well. Olga Pollatos (University of Munich, Germany) and colleagues studied anorectic females and showed that the perception of bodily signals assessed in heartbeat perception tests is decreased in anorexia nervosa. Women who were diagnosed with anorexia nervosa had deficits in recognizing certain visceral sensations related to hunger and satiety and exhibited a generally reduced capacity to accurately perceive cardiac signals [33].

Embodied choices are content and context dependent and thus the body does not play the same role in every kind of choice and in every situation. Content refers here to classes of choices that are made under conditions of either risk or uncertainty. Choices under risk, in contrast to choices under uncertainty, are made knowing the probabilities of success as well as the (monetary) value of all options. Whether and how gut feelings inform

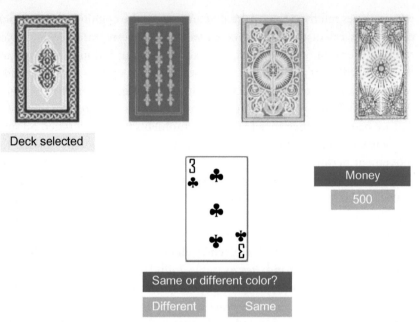

Fig. 3 Intuitive reasoning task used in Study 2. One each trial, participants chose one of four decks (top row) and then guessed if their card would be the same color as the upturned card (bottom row) or would be a different color. Increases and decreases in money won provided feedback as to whether or not guesses were correct. *(From B.D. Dunn, H.C. Galton, R. Morgan, D. Evans, C. Oliver, M. Meyer, R. Cusack, A.D. Lawrence, T. Dalgleish, Listening to your heart. How interoception shapes emotion experience and intuitive decision making, Psychol. Sci. 21 (12) (2010) 1835–1844, https://doi.org/10. 1177/0956797610389191. Epub 2010 Nov 24.).*

choices under risk and uncertainty differentially is mostly unknown. Context is another important factor in decision making, as a person's risk preference is not universal. The same person may prefer high risk in one domain (e.g., finance) and low risk in another (e.g., health or sports). Context has been well studied in choices under risk but less so in choices under uncertainty. Later, I will present examples of how individual differences define many of our embodied choices.

How do the gut and brain work together?

Recent reviews have summarized the paradigms and empirical findings that allow causal inference of bacteria–brain–behavior relationships [34]. For the causal effects of changes in the gut on human decision-making, most of the germ-free studies, animal studies, antibiotic-administration studies, transplant studies, and psychobiotic studies have shown that the gut actually does influence our choices without our knowing. One area that has received recent attention is the ingestion of probiotics [35]. Many companies advertise their benefits, but we must be careful to ask whether they are beneficial for all humans alike and for all choices we think may be affected by gut changes.

What do we know about probiotics and changes in behavior in humans? We know that providing humans with a probiotic mixture (vs a placebo) has reduced aggression and rumination [36]. Rumination, that is, thinking a lot about your past decisions and using a lot of deliberation when making decisions, has been shown to be a predictor of nonintuitive choices, which are based on deliberative processes [23]. Our own studies have shown that fast and accurate decisions can be achieved with low deliberation and a high preference for intuition [37]. In our lab, we used a decision-specific reinvestment scale that allowed us to psychometrically assess individual differences [38]. If you score high on a Reinvestment Scale you agree with questions such as "I'm always trying to figure out how I make decisions" that indicates that a person consciously monitors her decisions and if a person scores high on "I remember poor decisions I make for a long time afterwards," it indicates that he ruminates a lot in deciding.

We put athletes into high- or low-pressure situations and asked them to generate ideas to solve an ill-defined problem about how to continue an attack situation in which many possible options appeared to be appropriate. We measured their decision-specific reinvestment score and compared their decisions in the high- and low-pressure situations. Results showed that the decision-making performance of low- and high-decision reinvestors was similar in the low-pressure condition, but in the high-pressure condition, low reinvestors decided faster than the high reinvestors. This in itself confirms that if a situation causes you stress, relying on your intuition is beneficial, but it seems that not all players can easily do that. Although this appears to be a trait, other evidence has shown that it can be changed and that understanding how we physiologically cope with stress is an important way to go forward. Consider a physiological explanation, how we cope with stress that emphasize for the current physiological activity than a personality trait. The physiological explanation used the longest nerve in our body (Fig. 4): the vagus nerve. Vagus nerve connections are one of the important communication pathways between the bacteria, the brain, and the behavior.

Empirical evidence suggests that the vagus nerve, the 10th cranial nerve, serves as the coordinator of parasympathetic activity, one of two

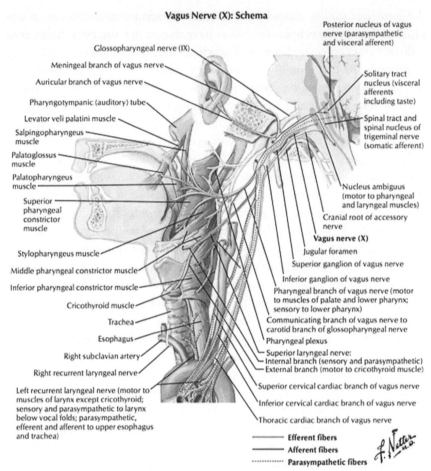

Vagus Nerve (X): Schema

Posterior nucleus of vagus nerve (parasympathetic and visceral afferent)

Glossopharyngeal nerve (IX)

Meningeal branch of vagus nerve

Auricular branch of vagus nerve

Pharyngotympanic (auditory) tube

Levator veli palatini muscle

Salpingopharyngeus muscle

Palatoglossus muscle

Palatopharyngeus muscle

Superior pharyngeal constrictor muscle

Stylopharyngeus muscle

Middle pharyngeal constrictor muscle

Inferior pharyngeal constrictor muscle

Cricothyroid muscle

Trachea

Esophagus

Right subclavian artery

Right recurrent laryngeal nerve

Left recurrent laryngeal nerve (motor to muscles of larynx except cricothyroid; sensory and parasympathetic to larynx below vocal folds; parasympathetic, efferent and afferent to upper esophagus and trachea)

Solitary tract nucleus (visceral afferents including taste)

Spinal tract and spinal nucleus of trigeminal nerve (somatic afferent)

Nucleus ambiguus (motor to pharyngeal and laryngeal muscles)

Cranial root of accessory nerve

Vagus nerve (X)

Jugular foramen

Superior ganglion of vagus nerve

Inferior ganglion of vagus nerve

Pharyngeal branch of vagus nerve (motor to muscles of palate and lower pharynx; sensory to lower pharynx)

Communicating branch of vagus nerve to carotid branch of glossopharyngeal nerve

Pharyngeal plexus

Superior laryngeal nerve:
Internal branch (sensory and parasympathetic)
External branch (motor to cricothyroid muscle)

Superior cervical cardiac branch of vagus nerve

Inferior cervical cardiac branch of vagus nerve

Thoracic cardiac branch of vagus nerve

——— Efferent fibers

——— Afferent fibers

·········· Parasympathetic fibers

Fig. 4 Anatomy of the proximal vagus nerve including branches. *(From H. Royden Jones, J. Srinivasan Jr., G. Allam, R. Baker, Cranial Nerves IX and X: Glossopharyngeal and Vagus In Netter's Neurology, second ed., 2011, p. 125 (Chapter 9). Image ID: 6963, © Elsevier Inc., Netterimages.com.).*

activities the autonomic nervous system switches between. The autonomic nervous system is responsible for regulating the body's unconscious actions. The parasympathetic system is responsible for stimulation resting activities that occur when the body is at rest and thus functioning in a relaxed way.

There are multiple ways to show that the vagus nerve activation is responsible for observed behavior by activating the parasympathetic system. For example, research paradigms have included psychopharmacology (changing the activation with drugs), vagotomy (removing parts of the vagus nerve), and vagus nerve stimulation (tickling the vagus nerve) [39]. If we tickle the vagus nerve at the ear, stimulation attenuates the inflammatory response to endotoxin [40] and thus provides a noninvasive method of manipulating the gut. At the same time, these stimulations are used to fight against pain, tinnitus, and other dysfunctions of the body, but the current research has yet to fulfill the long-awaited promise of using such methods to promote health.

How does the gut change your decisions?

Most studies have focused on regulation of emotions with changes in the gut, but recent work has explored how gut feelings change your embodied choices using both emotions and cognition. Recently, several of us in the Performance Psychology department at the German Sport University published a book on our research on the integration of cognition and emotions [41]. Other recent research on the interaction of microbiotics and cognition has involved learning and memory, two factors that have a long history in animal research, where clear functional and neurophysiological brain processes have been identified. In addition, research on the neurophysiological underpinnings of intuition [42] and creativity [43], among other concepts, has suggested that judgment and decision processes can be better understood as an interaction of brain processes and behavior [31].

Currently, it is not known whether there are just a few or many pathways between human traits and profiles and bacterial communities, or whether such relations are more trait or state in nature, given that (a) gut bacteria change over time and (b) situation-specific adaptations of intuitive choices have been reported [38]. As argued earlier, large-scale projects that have sufficient empirical power to understand gut and personality correlations are underway. If you want to know more about it, I highly recommend following updates on recent developments at the American Gut Project [44], the ELDERMET Project [45], and the Human Microbiome Project [46], which in addition to information provide self-assessments.

How does the gut affect your risky behavior?

Although the relation between the gut and choices has been identified in a number of studies, the benefits of intuitive choices themselves are often debated. For example, while benefits of intuition in conditions of uncertainty have been recognized [47], humans often try to avoid uncertainty entirely.

Intuitive choices are also not fully accepted in conditions of risk. No one has ever argued that chief executive officers (CEOs) should tell their shareholders that their decisions were based on some millisecond gut decision, and they will certainly not always rely on pure intuition. "I don't have reasons. I have instincts," said Sir Montagu Norman, governor of the Bank of England in the early 20th century. But you do not often hear today's CEOs quoting Sir Norman. Most bank managers, from small local banks to international institutions, are very sensitive to how they phrase future developments, given that they know how easily the stock market can be affected by a few wrongly interpreted sentences. Consider, for example, the chaotic changes in the world's stock markets that have occurred in response to one or another of President Donald Trump's Twitter messages.

One way CEOs could justify their reliance on intuition would be to make up a rational story for the public. Such a story might include reference to the wisdom of experts, or even the wisdom of the "inner crowd." The inner crowd describes the process of consulting yourself—making multiple estimates—before making a decision. Taking heed of the wisdom of the inner crowd has been recommended for monetary risk assessments. Just as Sir Francis Galton demonstrated the wisdom of crowds in estimating the weight of an ox, present-day researchers have shown that listening to one's inner crowd can also result in good choices [48]. Risk taking, however, not only varies by individual [49] but also depends on environmental factors. For example, in one comprehensive study, German and British participants both had a negative hardship index (index of economic difficulty, including, e.g., unemployment rate and changes in gas prices). Negative hardship index results are associated with a low homicide rate, high gross domestic product, low income inequality, low infant mortality, high life expectancy at birth, and high gender equality [50]. Nevertheless, it seems that German and British participants had quite different perspectives on the value of the United Kingdom's exit from the European Union (Brexit). Some of these differences in opinion may be biased by the information released by the press and politicians; others may be cultural differences based on the history of the countries. Other factors have much more to do with the individual; for example, gender and age have been shown to have a strong effect on risk taking in general [50].

Researchers have further emphasized the importance of using behavioral measures of risk and not solely relying on self-reports. Being cautious, banks often ask customers to report their investment risk preferences, since courts have made some banks responsible for the decisions of their clients. Are there other ways to gain this information that would be more embodied? What if clients were asked, with their own money in mind as their theoretical stake, to complete the balloon analogue risk task (often called BART)? The task involves pressing a button to inflate a balloon on a computer. With each button press the balloon gets bigger, and participants earn money with each pump. However, if the balloon explodes, they lose all their money. This is easily compared with the investments in the housing or stock market; bitcoins are similar. It turns out that this behavioral task shows quite a lot of individual differences that relate to other risk-taking behavior in general—and more than revealed in a self-report of low, medium, or high-risk tolerance.

A group of researchers in Vienna, Austria, showed that applying a driving test was much more beneficial for estimating risky driving in young people than self-reports [51]. Many of the rules governing insurance benefits (e.g., discounts for age or safe driving record) have been implemented partly on the basis of statistics and partly on these findings of risk-taking behavior that provide a better estimate of future risk taking. And the task can be much more embodied. For example, I once played the BART in a gaming shop in Costa Rica, in which a real balloon exploded in front of me when I pressed too much. An even more extreme version was played at a conference in Potsdam, Germany, where one of the speakers asked volunteers to blow up a balloon blindfolded. The largest inflated balloon would win a prize, and everyone could see just by looking at the faces of the volunteers that this was now very different from simply pressing a button to win a few cents.

To date, making decisions under risk and uncertainty has not been fully explored neurophysiologically, and current overviews of the neural pathways of decision-making do not entirely separate risk and uncertainty [52]. For example, Wim De Neys (French National Centre of Scientific Research) and Vinod Goel (York University, Canada) have argued that the neural basis of decision-making under risk and uncertainty can be found in the activation of the right lateral prefrontal cortex [53]. It has been argued that the lateral prefrontal cortex might inhibit inappropriate intuitions. Transcranial magnetic stimulation, which targets specific brain areas, may one day be used to inhibit areas involved in intuition [54], helping people who are prone to making impulsive choices. As argued earlier impulsive choices are not bad or good per se but in the earlier-mentioned example, we define them as inappropriate for reaching a better task performance. In short, manipulating the gut to influence embodied choices requires more research in the future, and it is very likely that those embodied choices vary by person, content, and context.

References

[1] D.R. Proffitt, M. Bhalla, R. Gossweiler, Perceiving geographical slant. Psychon. Bull. Rev. 2 (1995) 409, https://doi.org/10.3758/BF03210980.

[2] F.H. Durgin, J.A. Baird, M. Greenburg, R. Russell, K. Shaughnessy, S. Waymouth, Who is being deceived? The experimental demands of wearing a backpack. Psychon. Bull. Rev. 16 (5) (2009) 964–969, https://doi.org/10.3758/PBR.16.5.964.

[3] S. Maasen, W. Prinz, G. Roth (Eds.), Voluntary Action: Brains, Minds, and Sociality, Oxford University Press, London, UK, 2003.

[4] See in S. Goldin-Meadow, S.L. Beilock, Action's influence on thought: the case of gesture. Perspect. Psychol. Sci. 5 (2010) 664–674, https://doi.org/10.1177/1745691610388764.

[5] D. Casasanto, K. Jasmin, Good and bad in the hands of politicians: spontaneous gestures during positive and negative speech. PLoS One 5 (7) (2010) e11805, https://doi.org/10.1371/journal.pone.0011805.

[6] R.A. Carlson, M.N. Avraamides, M. Cary, S. Strasberg, What do the hands externalize in simple arithmetic, J. Exp. Psychol. Learn. Mem. Cogn. 33 (2007) 747–756.

[7] D. Casasanto, K. Dijkstra, Motor action and emotional memory. Cognition (2010). https://doi.org/10.1016/j.cognition.2009.11.002.

[8] J.M. Gottwald, B. Elsner, O. Pollatos, Good is up—spatial metaphors in action observation. Front. Psychol. (2015). https://doi.org/10.3389/fpsyg2015.01605.

[9] D. Liu, T. Verguts, M. Li, Z. Ling, Q. Chen, Dissociated spatial-arithmetic association in horizontal and vertical dimensions, Front. Psychol. 8 (2017) 1741.

[10] J. Löffler, M. Raab, R. Cañal-Bruland, Does movement influence representations of time and space? PLoS One 12 (4) (2017) 1–19.

[11] See the book of S. Beilock, How the Body Knows Its Mind, Atria Paperbooks, New York, NY, 2015.

[12] F. Strack, L.L. Martin, S. Stepper, Inhibiting and facilitating conditions of the human smile: a nonobtrusive test of the facial feedback hypothesis, J. Pers. Soc. Psychol. 54 (5) (1988) 768–777.

[13] E.-J. Wagenmakers, T. Beek, L. Dijkhoff, Q.F. Gronau, A. Acosta, R.B. Adams, et al., Registered replication report: Strack, Martin, & Stepper (1988), Perspect. Psychol. Sci. 11 (6) (2016) 917–928.

[14] T. Noah, Y. Schul, R. Mayo, When both the original study and its failed replication are correct: feeling observed eliminates the facial-feedback effect, J. Pers. Soc. Psychol. 114 (5) (2018) 657–664.

[15] M.C. Reimann, W. Feye, A.J. Malter, J.M. Ackerman, R. Castaño, N. Garg, … C.B. Zhong, Embodiment in judgment and choice. J. Neurosci. Psychol. Econ. 5 (2) (2012) 104–123, https://doi.org/10.1037/a0026855.

[16] S. Topolinski, R. Deutsch, Phasic affective modulation of creativity. Exp. Psychol. 59 (2012) 302–310, https://doi.org/10.1027/1618-3169/a000159.

[17] M. Raab, N. Green, Motion as input: a functional explanation of movement effects on cognitive processes, Percept. Mot. Skills 100 (2) (2005) 333–348.

[18] E.W. Carr, M. Rotteveel, P. Winkielman, Easy moves: perceptual fluency facilitates approach-related actions, Emotion 16 (2016) 540–552.

[19] S. Anderson, The Psychobiotic Revolution, National Geographic, Washington, DC, 2017.

[20] S. Danziger, J. Levav, L. Avnaim-Pesso, Extraneous factors in judicial decisions. Proc. Natl. Acad. Sci. 108 (17) (2011) 6889–6892, https://doi.org/10.1073/pnas.1018033108.

[21] A. Glöckner, The irrational hungry judge effect revisited: simulations reveal that the magnitude of the effect is overestimated, Judgm. Decis. Mak. 11 (6) (2016) 601–610.

[22] A. Glöckner, C.L.M. Witteman (Eds.), Foundations for Tracing Intuition: Challenges and Methods, Psychology Press & Routledge, London, 2010.

[23] C. Betsch, J.J. Kunz, Individual strategy preferences and decisional fit, J. Behav. Decis. Mak. 21 (2008) 532–555.

[24] D.E. Melnikoff, J.A. Bargh, The mythical number two. Trends Cogn. Sci. 22 (4) (2018) 280–293, https://doi.org/10.1016/j.tics.2018.02.001.

[25] K.G. Volz, L.J. Schooler, R.I. Schubotz, M. Raab, G. Gigerenzer, D.Y. von Cramon, Why you think Milan is larger than Modena: neural correlates of the recognition heuristic, J. Cogn. Neurosci. 18 (11) (2006) 1924–1936.

[26] A. Glöckner, T. Heinen, J.G. Johnson, M. Raab, Network approaches for expert decisions in sports, Hum. Mov. Sci. 31 (2012) 318–333.

[27] J.G. Johnson, M. Raab, Take the first: option-generation and resulting choices, Organ. Behav. Hum. Decis. Process. 91 (2) (2003) 215–229.

[28] D. Kahneman, G. Klein, Conditions for intuitive expertise. Am. Psychol. 64 (2009) 515–526, https://doi.org/10.1037/a0016755.

[29] M. Raab, Motor heuristics and embodied choices: how to choose and act. Curr. Opin. Psychol. 16 (2017) 34–37, https://doi.org/10.1016/j.copsyc.2017.02.029.

[30] M. Raab, SMART-ER: a situation model of anticipated response consequences in tactical decisions in skill acquisition—extended and revised. Front. Psychol. 5 (2015) https://doi.org/10.3389/fpsyg.2014.01533 [1533].

[31] P. Cisek, A. Pastor-Bernier, On the challenges and mechanisms of embodied decisions. Philos. Trans. R. Soc. B 369 (2014) 20130479, https://doi.org/10.1098/rstb.2013.0479.

[32] B.D. Dunn, H.C. Galton, R. Morgan, et al., Listening to your heart: how interoception shapes emotion experience and intuitive decision making, Psychol. Sci. 21 (2010) 1835–1844.

[33] O. Pollatos, A.L. Kurz, J. Albrecht, T. Schreder, A.M. Kleemann, V. Schöpf, et al., Reduced perception of bodily signals in anorexia nervosa, Eat. Behav. 9 (2008) 381–388.

[34] A. Sarkar, S. Harty, S.M. Letho, A.H. Moeller, T.G. Dinan, R.I.M. Dunbar, J.F. Cryan, P.W.J. Burnet, The microbiome in psychology and cognitive neuroscience, Trends Cogn. Sci. 22 (7) (2018) 611–636.

[35] F.Z. Marques, et al., Beyond gut feelings: how the gut microbiota regulates blood pressure, Nat. Rev. Cardiol. 15 (2018) 20.

[36] L. Steenbergen, et al., A randomized controlled trial to test the effect of multispecies probiotics on cognitive reactivity to sad mood, Brain Behav. Immun. 48 (2015) 258–264.

[37] M. Raab, S.J.P. Laborde, When to blink and when to think: preference for intuitive decisions results in faster and better tactical choices, Res. Q. Exerc. Sport 82 (1) (2011) 89–98.

[38] S. Laborde, M. Raab, N.P. Kinrade, Is the ability to keep your mind sharp under pressure reflected in your heart?: Evidence for the neurophysiological bases of decision reinvestment. Biol. Psychol. 100C (2014) 34–42, https://doi.org/10.1016/j.biopsycho.2014.05.003.

[39] L. Calzato, Theory-Driven Approaches to Cognitive Enhancement, Elsevier, Amsterdam, 2017.

[40] L.V. Borovikova, et al., Vagus nerve stimulation attenuates the systemic inflammatory response to endotoxin, Nature 405 (2000) 458–462.

[41] M. Raab, B. Lobinger, S. Hoffmann, A. Pizzera, S. Laborde, Performance Psychology. Perception, Action, Cognition, and Emotion, Academic Press, London, 2015.

[42] N.J. Horr, C. Braun, K.G. Volz, Feeling before knowing why: the role of the orbitofrontal cortex in intuitive judgments—an MEG study, Cogn. Affect. Behav. Neurosci. 14 (2014) 1271–1285.

[43] A. Dietrich, R. Kanso, A review of EEG, ERP and neuroimaging studies of creativity and insight, Psychol. Bull. 136 (2010) 822–848.

[44] http://humanproject.com/americangut/.

[45] http://eldermet.ucc.ie.

[46] https://hmpdacc.org.

[47] G. Gigerenzer, Gut Feelings. The Intelligence of the Unconscious, Viking, New York, 2007.

[48] S.M. Herzog, R. Hertwig, Harnessing the wisdom of the inner crowd, Trends Cogn. Sci. 18 (10) (2014) 504–506.

[49] R. Frey, A. Pedroni, R. Mata, J. Rieskamp, R. Hertwig, Risk preferences share the psychometric structure of major psychological traits, Sci. Adv. 3 (2017) e1701381.

[50] R. Mata, A.K. Josef, R. Hertwig, Propensity for risk taking across the life span and around the globe, Psychol. Sci. 27 (2) (2016) 231–243.

[51] A. Hergovich, M.E. Arendasy, M. Sommer, B. Bognar, The Vienna risk-taking test—traffic. A new measure of road traffic risk-taking, J. Individ. Differ. 28 (2007) 198–204.

[52] O. Vartanian, D.R. Mandel, Neuroscience of Decision Making, Taylor and Francis, New York, 2011.

[53] W. De Neys, V. Goel, Heuristics and biases in the brain: dual neural pathways for decision making, in: O. Vartanian, D.R. Mandel (Eds.), Neuroscience of Decision Making, Psychology Press, Taylor and Francis Group, New York, Hove, 2011, pp. 125–141.

[54] C. Brevet-Aeby, J. Brunelin, S. Iceta, et al., Prefrontal cortex and impulsivity: interest of noninvasive brain stimulation, Neurosci. Biobehav. Rev. 71 (2016) 112–134.

CHAPTER FIVE

Action enables perception and cognition and thus embodied choices

Catching a flying ball after some training seems quite easy, but have you seen robots catching fly balls? It is a mess! It often only works if the robot stands still [1], clearly rendering them not yet ready for baseball outfields, but why? One reason is that robots have often used only one sensory input—vision— and too much visual sensory information in this case. But if robots use both vision and information for their own movements, they perform much better, as recently demonstrated by a robot called Puppy [2]. Thus action enables perception is often called an intelligence that is not minor in comparison to other intelligences. Stephen Jay Gould after his PhD at Columbia University in the United States wrote: "we tend to characterize the mental skill of athletes as an intuitive grasp of bodily movement and position—a 'physical intelligence,' if you will" [3].

Every day it seems we see progress in human-like cognition in robots. But how do humans catch balls? Interestingly the way most textbooks explain how humans do it is very different from how robots catch balls. It seems the robots' programs use a lot of information that humans actually do not, such as predicting the flight curve, the landing point, and much more. Humans simply run in the direction of the ball while keeping the ball speed constant in the visual field, often called optical acceleration cancelation. Adjusting your speed while running toward a flying ball will result in being at the place where the ball will land. This so-called outfielder problem, as Andy Clark from the University of Edinburgh called it a simple example of how adapting movement can result in a good outcome. Deciding on a running speed is a matter of adjusting to changes in the acceleration in the visual field, and slowing down or speeding up are the two options to take. From an embodied choice perspective as introduced in Chapter 1, outfielders use the simple gaze heuristic. As Gerd Gigerenzer from the Max Planck Institute of Human Development in Berlin explained in his book on gut feelings, instead of performing complex calculations on the basis

Judgment, Decision-Making, and Embodied Choices
https://doi.org/10.1016/B978-0-12-823523-2.00005-2

47

of some information, simply keep your gaze constant and you will end up with a good decision using one simple cue.

You cannot imagine how many papers have been written about catching balls, and yes, the story may be more complicated. For example, the gaze heuristic cannot be used if the ball flies straight at you and not as a high-arcing ball, as when a batter hits the ball back to the pitcher in baseball. However, as discussed in a chapter Gigerenzer and I published some years ago, you can apply a different heuristic, the time-to-contact heuristic [4]. The time-to-contact mechanisms for catching a fly ball were proposed by vision researchers Peter McLeod and Zoltan Dienes (Oxford University, England) [5]. They used a well-known phenomenon: As an object, in this case a ball, approaches you, the projection of the ball in the retina will increase and the ball will appear larger and larger. That change in size is used to estimate when the ball will land in your eye—and you will prepare to avoid that by catching, defending, or diving, depending on the sport. This principle has been shown to work quite efficiently in humans for many movements, such as deciding to increase your running speed when trying to hit the takeoff board for a long jump or to catch a ball [6]. Time-to-contact is hardwired in the body and that is why it is not an abstract cognition, that is, a request to calculate or make complex decisions. An embodied choice is what it is. The hardwired connection goes from the eye to groups of neurons in the brain, as studies in birds showed. Nor does the time-to-contact principle apply exclusively to humans. For birds, as you can imagine, it is quite important to know when they will hit the water as they dive to catch a fish so they can fold their wings to the body at the right time. It is a quite demanding timing task: not too early, to make sure to control their direction, and not too late, to make sure they do not break their wings [7].

Both the gaze heuristic and the time-to-contact heuristic illustrate nicely that the body is capable of making embodied choices. You might use one or the other heuristic depending on what information is available: Keep your gaze constant when running, or use the changing size of an approaching object when it is coming straight at you. Our bodies are quite well adapted to changes in the environment. For example, it is quite hard to tell me what temperature you want the water to be for your bath, but you are very sensitive to changes, such as the water becoming too hot or too cold.

For most existing objects, we are quite good at estimating sizes and often we use changes rather than absolute size, but the brain can trick us. For example, have you heard of the moon illusion? According to Wikipedia, this is "an optical illusion which causes the Moon to appear larger near the

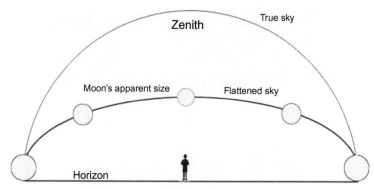

Fig. 1 Moon perception. *(From https://skyandtelescope.org/observing/moon-illusion-confusion11252015/, Illustration by Bob King; Adapted from L. Kaufman, J.H. Kaufman, Explaining the moon illusion, Proc. Natl. Acad. Sci. 97 (1) (2000) 500–505, https://doi. org/10.1073/pnas.97.1.500; Copyright (2000) National Academy of Sciences, U.S.A.).*

horizon than it does higher up in the sky (Fig. 1). It has been known since ancient times and recorded by various cultures" [8].

Of course, we call it an illusion because the object appears to be larger near the horizon, but we assume that the size of the moon is constant. The explanation of this illusion is hotly debated and some of the explanations have to do with the context, for example, the moon is perceived relative to other objects, say, near the horizon or a boat or a house. Other explanations have to do with our experience with objects: We have nothing of that size on earth and could not walk around it. Other arguments say it depends on personal visual experiences as well. If you are used to observing distant objects and need to estimate their size, you may be better at overcoming the illusion. Interestingly the visual system is easily tricked by illusions but embodied choices are not. When I was in the ocean in Costa Rica a large manta ray approached me. The first thing that came to my mind was "somebody died recently; who was that again?" but I focused on the object and remembered that objects under water look larger and closer than they actually are. I have to say that knowledge did not help me much. I just stood still until the manta ray made a turn and vanished. This example, however, illustrates another illusion of size and distance. How can we measure that in embodied choices these illusions disappear?

Let us consider the Müller-Lyer illusion: Two lines of identical length are presented, but at the ends of one line are arrows whose fins point in toward the line and at the ends of the other line are arrows whose fins point outward.

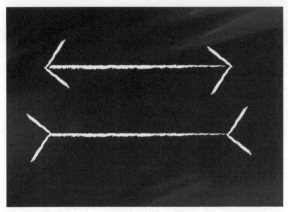

Fig. 2 The Müller-Lyer illusion. Is one line longer than the other, or are they the same length?

Even if you know the illusion and you know both lines are the same length you cannot overcome the feeling that the line with the arrows turned outward is larger (the lower line in Fig. 2). However, if an experimenter asked you to grab the line with your index finger and thumb, the opening between your digits would reflect the length of the line, revealing that you are not buying the illusion [9]. But other findings, such as from Volker Franz from the University Göttingen in Germany, suggest that the action system can also be tricked. I argued earlier that embodied choices use bodily information, but in no way am I suggesting that they are always correct or never influenced by early perceptual information.

Knowledge about these illusions can help to improve embodied choices. Let us consider the worldwide disease of overweight and obesity. It seems that simply reminding people to exercise or warning them about health issues if they do not take the stairs instead of the elevator is not an effective way to activate moving. What would researchers of embodied choices do instead? One example I like a lot is something my colleague Rich Masters and his group have done in Hong Kong. They simply moved the stair banister slightly by about 2 degrees, so that it either diverged or converged with the stairs. When the banister converged (vs diverged) with the stairs, participants thought it was less steep. In a second study, walking speed was significantly slower when the banister diverged from, rather than converged with, the stairs [10]. Masters argued that changing the built environment in this way could lead to safer stair descent or even, if the stairs are not perceived to be as steep, to more people taking the stairs than an elevator. They will be exploring these possibilities in further studies, and I hope the results show that this simple manipulation works to change behavior. The logic of it follows the idea that changes in the environment produce perceptual illusions that allow embodied choices to take over.

Changing the environment to encourage moving has many looks. On YouTube you will find videos of cities that have built sound into the stairs. Each step plays a note, so a person moving up and down produces music [11]. Of course, health psychology and exercise psychology are full of good ideas, such as buying a dog so you will walk more. Carrie Westgarth (University of Liverpool, England) surveyed dog owners and found that walking your dog makes you happier and improves your health [12]. I have two dogs, and the daily hassle of convincing my kids to walk with me and the dog even when it is dark or rainy does not fully subjectively support the general effect of these findings, but I do see the point. I also admit sometimes it is really me that does not get the kick to getting the dogs out, but walking the dogs with my kids buys us time together without the distraction of a smartphone or tablet, and this invariably makes me happier. The neurophysiological underpinnings of such subjective feelings are well studied. Recently, it has been found that a specific hormone (oxytocin) is released in both the human and the dog when interacting [13]. This hormone is well known as the "love hormone" or the "bonding hormone" (e.g., in breast-feeding babies). Brian Hare from Duke University in the United States showed that oxytocin is also released in dogs' brains when they are petted or when the dogs are looking at their owners [14].

When I wrote this I was in Hamilton, New Zealand, at the University of Waikato on the North Island. Every day I went for coffee and lunch to the campus's nice lake and coffee shops and I realized how naturally the walking path was integrated into the curves and flows and the ups and downs of the terrain. It took me some time to realize that this is very different from in Europe, where a campus path between two points often follows a straight line and if it does not, you see in the grass the shortcuts people have taken that produce the shortest possible distance. In New Zealand, I did not see so many shortcuts, and I realized I walked more because the paths followed the characteristics of the original landscape. When walking in this landscape I found myself not even trying to take a shortcut. When I returned to my office at the Faculty of Health, Sport, and Human Performance I read that my home university, the German Sport University of Cologne, would be hosting the European Forum on Urban Forestry. I hope the outcome of this and similar meetings will encourage cities to improve embodied choices by providing opportunities for our health without our minds even knowing.

By the way, the paths that followed the curves and other natural features of the landscape on the Waikato campus were not unique. The river walk in Hamilton also follows the natural flow of the rolling hills. Even the hobbit houses built into the hills that I saw on my tourist tour showed me a different way we could nurture ourselves in nature [15].

Actions enable social interactions

I once walked down the hall with a colleague after an important and long meeting, fully exhausted and just looking down and not talking. Later another colleague came to me and said she was so sorry that we had not been successful in achieving the goal of our meeting, which I had earlier told her was so important to me. Surprised, I told her everything was fine and we had achieved what we wanted, and I wondered why she thought this was not so. She replied that she had assumed this was the case because I had passed her a sad look in the hall, not even seeing that she was passing by. This indeed can happen: Having one's head down can be interpreted as being unhappy rather than tired, and not greeting someone can been perceived as arrogance or disinterest rather than distraction, even if this is not at all true. Thus actions can be perceived by others as expressions of the inner state. Or as Evan Thompson at the University of British Columbia, Canada said once: "We experience the other directly as a person, that is, as an intentional and mental being whose bodily gestures and actions are expressive of his or her experiences and states of mind" (p. 264) [16]. We even ascribe human qualities to actions of nonhumans, as Hollywood has long put to profitable use in their animated movies. For example, in a study by Peter Todd (now at Indiana University, United States) and colleagues, when participants were presented with two dots moving on a screen, they attributed intentions to these dots, such as one was chasing the other or they were playing together. Actions of others are sometimes interpreted correctly and some-times not. Understanding action intentions by observation and expressing your "inner self" by your movements serve a larger goal in our development, as argued by Wolfgang Prinz (Leipzig, Germany) in his book *Open Minds* [17]. He suggested actions are an important way to build your own identity and become a social person. Empathy, from the German word *Einfühlung* (first introduced by Theodor Lipp in 1907 and later translated by Titchener in 1909), refers to an affective state that allows us to put ourselves in someone else's shoes. Empathy has been well differentiated from emotional conta-gion, sympathy, and mindreading [18], but for now it is sufficient to use empathy as an example. It seems that our motor experience helps us build empathy and correctly interpret the intentions of others by their movements. A colleague, Vassilis Sevdalis that was a post doc at German Sport University Cologne and now is at Aarhus University in Denmark and I conducted a study in which participants with different amounts of sports experience viewed point-light displays, that is, 13 moving dots representing a person dancing. The dancing movements were selected from a database of expressive or nonexpressive dance movements and we simply asked participants to rate how expressive each of the dance movements presented as a cloud of dots was. Participants with a more extensive sports history were better at judging expressiveness than those with a shorter history. As discussed earlier, one is able to imagine oneself making similar movements and thus is able to categorize them according to one's own bodily experience. These judgments are the evidence of embodied choices [19].

Understanding actions of others is key to achieving something with another person, often called joint actions. Joint actions are a showcase for how actions enable joint behavior. More than synchronization, such as when people automatically coordinate their swings in two rocking chairs, joint action here means sharing a goal and intending to jointly act on it. Consider the case of two people lifting a large plank of wood by touching it only at the ends. It seems that we somehow consider the action of the other when putting our movements in place. Michael J. Richardson and colleagues (University of Connecticut, United States) found that we behave as if we have considered the arm length of the other person with whom we lift objects of different lengths [20]. Other studies have shown that we consider the strength of the other person or the way someone may move an object that is lifted together. Those decisions are probably embodied choices that do not calculate details of the other's movement. Most likely the joint action is successfully completed because we represent and share the intentions and goals of the other but then use our observations of the other's movements to adapt our movements in such a way that we are able to lift an object. It appears that the cognitive system is sometimes too slow and unable to process how to make these choices by pure cognition.

Another example that comes to mind is a jazz quartet I happened to see in a jazz lounge in Hamilton, New Zealand. They started together and had some basic shared intentions, but as they took turns soloing it became clear the others reacted to the soloist and each other in a way that sustained the song but was unlikely to have been preplanned. You can observe the same pattern of dynamics in invasion sports when teams do have some strategies to open an attack but the little details and joint actions simply evolve from the embodied choices and dynamics of the team members and opponents in the heat of the moment.

So how do people act jointly? It looks as if they share a socially defined intention but they may not need to fully represent the social agent when performing, as Roman Liepelt, a colleague in my department, has shown with a group of researchers from Leipzig, Germany. They showed that non-social attentional saliency could explain the ease with which joint actions are often performed. The asked pairs of participants to perform a joint Simon task, in which one of the participants is asked to act on only one dimension of a stimulus on a computer, such as press the left button when a number displayed is larger than 5, while the other person is tasked with pressing the right button when numbers are smaller than 5. In the classic Simon task, this is done by one person and the person has slower reactions when the stimulus is, for example, presented on the left side but the right button has to be pressed, as the spatial location of the stimulus and the response are noncongruent. But it seems the Simon effect occurs even in a joint situation in which a person is responsible for only one side of the response. It has been argued that a person simply mentally activates the other side's responses and this slows down that person's responses. The group in Leipzig also showed that the effect can be induced not only when a person sits next to the participant, sharing the task of pressing left and right buttons when stimuli appear on the screen, but also when, for example, a Japanese waving cat or a ticking metronome is present [21]. However, simply describing the other actions as affordances, which I discussed earlier, that socially impel a person to specific actions does not seem to be able to explain many different kinds of joint actions, as one person's part of a joint action sometimes need to deviate from the partner's actions to arrive at the shared goal. It seems important how our body influence choices in the context of joint actions and there are many other examples such as coworking in industry or playing beach volleyball.

One prominent explanation of how action enables social interaction comes from the field of embodied simulation. In short, it relies heavily on so-called mirror neurons, which were first detected in monkeys. Monkey mirror neurons fire when a monkey produces a grasping movement and when observing a grasping movement of an experimenter or another monkey. Given that we can simulate the observed action, we can also infer the goal of the action, which in turn may give us a window on the other's intentions or feelings. Mirror neurons have been found to exist for other senses such as hearing and for eye movements, which enable shared attention [22]. Developmental scientists have argued that to understand others' goals, children from early on capitalize on their own motor experiences. For example, in a study by Jessica A. Sommerville from the University of Washington Seattle, United States, and colleagues, children at the age of just 3 months were able to identify goals of others in an action sequence but only to the extent that they themselves were able to perform the actions [23]. The same results were found in gaze strategies and grasping; children's gaze strategies for predicting others' actions correlated with their own motor skills [24]. Finally, consider studies on false-belief tests [25]: Paula Rubio-Fernandez from London and colleagues developed a so-called Duplo test for 3-year-old children. This test has two phases. In the first phase, children are familiarized with several Duplo items: a girl figure, a bunch of bananas, and two little cupboards. The children hear a story about the little girl loving bananas for her breakfast. Playing out a scene with the Duplo, the experimenter has the girl figure put the bananas into one of the cupboards and then tells the children that the little girl wants to go for a walk, turning the girl figure's back to the scene. The children see the girl in front of themselves and see that the girl is unable to see the scene. This understanding is confirmed by asking the children if the girl can see where the experimenter is behind her back and in the scene. Only then does the experimenter move the bananas from the cupboard they are in to the other cupboard. Again, the experimenter asks the children if the girl has seen what the experimenter has done to confirm the girl figure's perspective in the scene. Finally, the experimenter asks whether the children want to play with the little girl and turns the girl back to the scene, asking, "what is the girl going to do next?" In the studies from Paula Rubio-Fernandez and colleagues, 80% of the 3-year-old children had the girl open the now-empty cupboard, understanding that this is where the girl would look to find the bananas. This is in contrast to only 23% of children in a classic false-belief task in which a puppet leaves the room and children have not played with the puppet before and then children are asked as above. Most important for embodied choices, when the children were not allowed to interact with the Duplo girl, the success rate fell to 22%, indicating that activating social interaction with movements increases the understanding of others' perspectives [26].

Taken together, these studies suggest that our own experience of our motor system enables us to detect intentions of others via their movements. Because we are most familiar with our own motor behavior, it is not surprising, then, that playing a duet with a virtual partner at the piano works best when the sound of the virtual partner is actually a previous recording of yourself rather than some other person, as Peter Keller from the University of Sydney, Australia, and colleagues found out [27].

Do muscles have intelligence? The case of motor intentionality

A new term that has been recently introduced is Motor intentionality. Motor intentionality seems to require some intelligence in the motor system. Of course, no one is suggesting that each of our muscles is intelligent in a psychological sense with a measured IQ score, but somehow, we are able to change our movement patterns without much thinking, as when we orient our grasp depending on if we want to move a glass or use it for drinking. In the section on gestures, we also saw a strong relation between language and the body that seems to be shaped by evolution. From gesturing, we may have developed speech in the stone age, as this enabled us to use our hands for other tasks or tools.

One piece of evidence of this is that the monkey's brain areas for the motor system through evolution became in humans what we call the Broca's area, which is dedicated to language [28]. The Broca's area in humans is still active in movement preparation, or action sequencing. For example, presentation of the word "lick" to people activates the motor homunculus of the tongue that does the licking [29]. This relation may explain why eating popcorn or chewing gum (so-called oral interference) during the advertisements before a movie in a cinema reduces the amount spent on these advertised products a week later. Further, if participants are asked about their preferences for brands that have been either presented before the movie or not the control group that did not eat popcorn or chew gum spend more money or liked brands more that have been presented before the movie whereas the participants eating popcorn or chewing gum did not show any preference differences between presented or not presented brands (Fig. 3) [30].

It seems that language is highly related to the body, from gestures to the vocal system producing the sounds we socialized as communication. For example, metaphors not only enable communication between speakers but also are inherently grounded in meaning for the body. It is indeed fascinating that just the mere weight of a clipboard can influence the ratings of the value for an currency (Fig. 4).

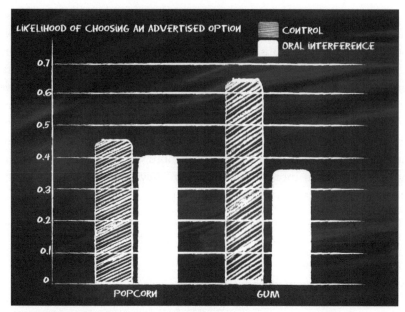

Fig. 3 Likelihood of choosing an advertised product in the oral interference condition (popcorn vs gum) in comparison with a control/no interference condition.

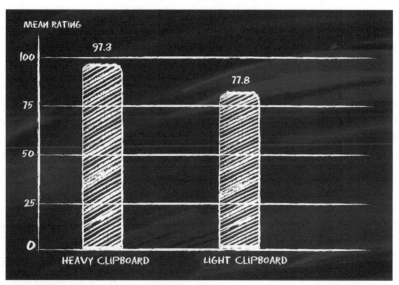

Fig. 4 Ratings for the value of currencies ranging from 0 to 200 cents, depending on the weight of the clipboard (heavy vs light).

Mark Johnson showed why we equate "important" with "big" or say "more" is "up," or why "activities" are "motions" or "causes" are "forces" and many more [31]. Consider one example: A study by Nils B. Jostmann (University of Amsterdam, Netherlands) and colleagues showed that students who were told a book was important judged it to be physically heavier than one they were told was unimportant. The interpretation of the finding is based on George Lakoff's conceptual metaphor theory indicating that when something is important, it is heavy. In a further study by the same authors, participants judged a currency as more valuable and their opinions and their leaders as more important when they answered questions on a heavy clipboard than on a light clipboard [32].

Embodied choices influenced by the environment

You remember the Danzinger study discussed earlier, in which judges' favorable rulings dropped from 65% to near zero from the early morning to just before lunch and went back up to 65% after lunch. Well maybe it is not all about the microbiota in the gut changing gut feelings. Maybe the room gets warmer and warmer until lunch, when they come back from lunch the room was as cool as in the morning again. My point is that temperature in a room may change judges' decisions as well, and even though as yet there is no empirical evidence, temperature has been thought to account for some of the judgments in court [33] and to be part of the increasing confidence in the fairness of the justice system [34]. Why do people think this may be so? Well, most of the arguments are based on empirical research showing that temperature changes judgments, impulsivity, and aggression. For example, Christine Gockel from the SRH Applied University Berlin, Germany and colleagues asked participants to infer criminality and criminal intent of criminals shown to them as pictures. Participants in a room with a low temperature judged the crime to be premediated and therefore deserving of a more severe penalty—as if the temperature primed them to perceive the criminals as "cold-hearted." In contrast, the participants in a room with a high temperature were primed to think of the criminals as "hot-headed" and thus ascribed impulsivity to the crimes (Fig. 5) [35].

In a similar manner, temperature can change the way we interact with others, feel empathy, or make moral decisions. For example, in a study by Lawrence E. Willams (University of Colorado, United States) and John A. Bargh (Yale University, United States), participants had either a warm or a cold drink in their hands. When asked to rate people, those participants

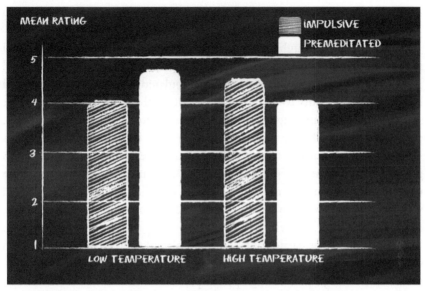

Fig. 5 Ratings in rooms with a low vs high temperature on the impulsiveness and pre-meditation of crimes.

holding a warm drink rated people as emotionally warmer than those hold-ing a cold drink. In another study by the same authors, participants with the warm drink preferred to give a reward for study participation to a friend, whereas the participants with the cold drink preferred to keep it for them-selves [36]. Note that these findings are sometimes hard to replicate and thus the current evidence cannot allow to generate these findings [37].

Social interactions can also be influenced by bodily experience that are very subtle. Imagine you are shopping for a new car and you are sitting on either a hard-wooden chair or a soft cushioned chair. Would that change your negotiation with a car dealer? It seems it does, as Joshua M. Ackerman from the Sloan School of Management, Massachusetts Institute of Technol-ogy, United States, and colleagues found out in an experiment in which par-ticipants had their first offer rejected by the dealer. Those sitting in a hard chair conceded less from the first to the second offer. The hardness of the seat activated an unrelated negotiation behavior that matched the partici-pants' comfort level: They held a harder line in the negotiation [38]. The same effect was found in a different study in which sitting in a hard chair caused participants to recommend harsher sentences for perpetrators in a criminal scenario. Like the decisions of judges before and after lunch, this is another example that even quite important decisions are not always based purely on a cognitive analysis—the body plays its role [39].

Even touching rough materials increased the perception that a social interaction such as playing the ultimatum game may become rough and adversarial. Ackerman and colleagues manipulated the touching of material by asking participants to complete a puzzle with pieces that were either smooth or covered in rough sandpaper. Directly after completing the puzzle, participants were asked to play an ultimatum game in which one participants would receive 10 tickets for a $50 lottery and had to decide how many to give to an anonymous (confederate of the experimenter) participant. The other participant supposedly would decide whether to accept the offer, in which case both decision makers would keep their respective allocations, or reject the offer, in which case both participants would get nothing. Results showed that participants who had played with a rough rather than smooth puzzle offered more tickets in the ultimatum game. This was interpreted as meaning that the rough puzzle pieces activated the belief in a rough social interaction and thus a higher offer would produce a higher likelihood of acceptance of their offer.

Another study revealed that moral decisions can be influenced by temperature as well. Hiroko Nakamura (Nagoya University, Japan) and colleagues ran two studies in which they showed that putting people in a cold room reduced their empathic judgments and facilitated more utilitarian judgments when they had to decide whether they should sacrifice a few people to achieve the greater good for others [40]. A classic dilemma is the so-called trolley dilemma. Participants are asked whether they would push an innocent person on a footbridge into the path of a runaway trolley and kill that one person to save five other lives [41]. The authors concluded that coldness biases people toward being "cold-hearted," reduces empathetic concern, and facilitates utilitarian moral judgments that see the utility of the sacrifice of one for the good of many. Likewise, Seung H. Lee (Colorado State University, United States) and colleagues reported that consumers perceived the ambient temperature to be cooler when eating alone than when eating with a partner [42]. Temperature also increases the impulsivity of humans, and you may have perceived this when, on vacation in a very hot and humid environment, you find yourself, tired from travel, in a space packed full of people. I remember my first time in Hong Kong, completely soaked in sweat and bone tired, I really had a hard time with my self-control when jostled by people in a crowded boat or tram. My judgments of intentionality when someone bumped into me were affected. Ordinarily an easy-going guy, I came to think the bumps were on purpose. In hindsight, I think the collisions were not intentional but at that moment, they felt like it!

My colleagues Nadia Gaoua and Rita de Oliveira (London South Bank University) and I recently predicted that at the 2022 FIFA World Cup in Qatar, referees will give more foul warnings and yellow cards to the teams for two reasons: First, the heat will cause the referees themselves to increase their impulsive judgments. Complex cognitive performance in hot environments may be influenced by the feelings of displeasure induced by rapid increases in skin temperature [43]. Second, the impulsivity of the players will rise. If the temperature increases physical fatigue and the displeasure of being fouled, revenge fouls are more likely. We will see whether the recent change of moving the World Cup toward fall in Qatar will reduce the temperature as much that it can reduce such effects.

References

[1] https://www.youtube.com/watch?v=R6pPwP3s7s4.

[2] Matej Hoffmann and Rolf Pfeifer inA. Newen, L. De Bruin, S. Gallagher (Eds.), The Oxford Handbook of 4E Cognition, Oxford Press, Oxford, UK, 2018, pp. 841–861.

[3] J.S. Gould, The Brain of Brawn, (2000) 1. Retrieved from: 24 March 2020, https://www.nytimes.com/2000/06/25/opinion/the-brain-of-brawn.html.

[4] M. Raab, G. Gigerenzer, Intelligence as smart heuristics, in: Cognition and Intelligence: Identifying the Mechanisms of the Mind, Cambridge University Press, New York, 2005, pp. 188–207.

[5] P. McLeod, Z. Dienes, Do fielders know where to go to catch the ball or only how to get there? J. Exp. Psychol. Hum. Percept. Perform. 22 (1996) 531–543.

[6] G.J.P. Savelsbergh, H.T.A. Whiting, R.J. Bootsma, Grasping tau, J. Exp. Psychol. Hum. Percept. Perform. 17 (1991) 315–322.

[7] Y. Wang, B.J. Frost, Time to collision is signaled by neurons in the nucleus rotundus of pigeons, Nature 356 (1992) 236–238.

[8] https://en.wikipedia.org/wiki/Moon_illusion.

[9] S. Aglioti, J.F.X. DeSouza, M.A. Goodale, Size-contrast illusions deceive the eye but not the hand, Curr. Biol. 5 (1995) 679–685.

[10] R. Masters, C. Capio, J. Poolton, L. Uiga, Perceptual modification of the built environment to influence behavior associated with physical activity: quasi-experimental field studies of a stair banister illusion. Sports Med. (2018) https://doi.org/10.1007/s40279-018-0869-5.

[11] https://www.youtube.com/watch?v=2lXh2n0aPyw.

[12] C. Westgarth, R.M. Christley, G. Marvin, E. Perkins, I walk my dog because it makes me happy: a qualitative study to understand why dogs motivate walking and improved health, Int. J. Environ. Res. Public Health 14 (2017) 936.

[13] B. Hare, M. Brown, C. Williamson, M. Tomasello, The domestication of social cognition in dogs, Science 298 (2002) 1634–1636.

[14] See more on dog intelligence at https://www.dognition.com from Brian Hare and other researchers.

[15] https://www.hobbitontours.com/en/our-story/.

[16] E. Thomson, Empathy and human experience, in: J. Proctor (Ed.), Science Religion, and the Human Experience, Oxford University Press, New York, 2005, pp. 260–285.

[17] W. Prinz, Open Minds. The Social Making of Agency and Intentionality, MIT Press, MA, USA, 2012.

[18] E. de Vignemont, P. Jacob, What is it like to feel anothers' pain, Philos. Sci. 79 (2) (2012) 295–316.

[19] V. Sevdalis, M. Raab, Individual differences in athletes' perception of expressive body movements. Psychol. Sport Exerc. 24 (2016) 111–117, https://doi.org/10.1016/j.psychsport. 2016.02.001.

[20] M.J. Richarsdson, K.L. Marsh, R.M. Baron, Judging and actualizing interpersonal and interpersonal affordances, J. Exp. Psychol. Hum. Percept. Perform. 23 (4) (2007) 845–859.

[21] T. Dolk, B. Hommel, L.S. Colzato, S. Schütz-Bosbach, W. Prinz, R. Liepelt, The joint Simon effect: a review and theoretical integration. Front. Psychol. 5 (2014) https://doi.org/10.3389/fpsyg. 2014.00974 Article ID 974.

[22] S.V. Shepherd, J.T. Klein, R.O. Deaner, M.I. Platt, Mirroring attention by neurons in monkey parietal cortex, Proc. Natl. Acad. Sci. 106 (23) (2009) 9489–9494.

[23] J.A. Sommerville, A. Woodward, Pulling out the intentional structure of action; the relation between action-processing and action production in infancy, Cognition 95 (1) (2005) 1–30.

[24] E. Ambrosini, V. Reddy, A. de Looper, M. Costantini, B. Lopez, C. Sinigaglia, Looking ahead: anticipatory gaze and motor ability in infancy. PLoS One 8 (7) (2013) e67916, https://doi.org/10.1371/journal.pone.0067916.

[25] See for an overview Leon de Bruin inA. Newen, L. De Bruin, S. Gallagher (Eds.), The Oxford Handbook of 4E Cognition, Oxford Press, Oxford, UK, 2018, pp. 493–512.

[26] P. Rubio-Fernandez, B. Geurts, How to pass the false-belief task before our fourth birthday, Psychol. Sci. 24 (2013) 27–33.

[27] P.E. Keller, G. Knoblich, B.H. Repp, Pianists duet better when they play with themselves: on the possible role of action simulation in synchronization, Conscious. Cogn. 16 (2007) 102–111.

[28] See Shaun GallagherA. Newen, L. De Bruin, S. Gallagher (Eds.), The Oxford Handbook of 4E Cognition, Oxford Press, Oxford, UK, 2018, pp. 353–367.

[29] E. Pulvermüller, Brain mechanisms linking language and action, Nat. Rev. Neurosci. 6 (2005) 576–582.

[30] S. Topolinski, S. Lindner, A. Freudenberg, Popcorn in the cinema: oral interference sabotages advertising effects. J. Consum. Psychol. 24 (2014) 169–176, https://doi.org/10.1016/j.jcps.2013.09.008.

[31] Mark Johnson inA. Newen, L. De Bruin, S. Gallagher (Eds.), The Oxford Handbook of 4E Cognition, Oxford Press, Oxford, UK, 2018, pp. 623–639.

[32] N.B. Jostmann, D. Lakens, T.W. Schubert, Weight as an embodiment of importance, Psychol. Sci. 1 (2009) 1169–1174.

[33] A. Benforado, The body of the mind: embodied cognition, law and justice, St. Louis Univ. Law J. 54 (2009) 1185.

[34] In Somogy Varga inA. Newen, L. De Bruin, S. Gallagher (Eds.), The Oxford Handbook of 4E Cognition, Oxford Press, Oxford, UK, 2018, pp. 863–874.

[35] C. Gockel, P.M. Kolb, L. Werth, Murder or not? Cold temperature makes criminals appear to be cold-blooded and warm temperature to be hot-headed, PLoS One 9 (4) (2014) e96231.

[36] L.E. Williams, J.A. Bargh, Experiencing physical warmth promotes interpersonal warmth, Science 322 (2008) 606–607.

[37] A. Altmejd, A. Dreber, E. Forsell, J. Huber, T. Imai, M. Johannesson, et al., Predicting the replicability of social science lab experiments. PLoS One 14 (12) (2019) e0225826, https://doi.org/10.1371/journal.pone.0225826.

[38] J.M. Ackerman, C.C. Nocera, J.A. Bargh, Incidental haptic sensations influence social judgments and decisions, Science 328 (2010) 1712–1715.

[39] L. Cherkasskiy, H. Song, S. Malahy, J.A. Bargh, Soft on crime: sitting in soft versus hard chairs produces more lenient recommended sentences. Hot topic talk at the embodiment preconference of the Society for Personality and Social Psychology, San Diego, CA, (2012, January).

[40] N. Hiroko, I. Yuichi, H. Yoshiko, M. Takuya, J. Kawaguchi, Cold-hearted or cool-headed: physical coldness promotes utilitarian moral judgment. Front. Psychol. 5 (2014) 1086, https://doi.org/10.3389/fpsyg.2014.01086.

[41] J.J. Thomson, Killing, letting die, and the trolley problem, Monist 59 (1976) 204–217.

[42] S.H.M. Lee, J.D. Rotman, A.W. Perkins, Embodied cognition and social consumption: self-regulating temperature through social products and behaviors, J. Consum. Psychol. 24 (2) (2014) 234–240.

[43] N. Gaoua, J. Grantham, S. Racinais, F. El Massioui, Sensory displeasure reduces cognitive performance in the heat, J. Environ. Psychol. 32 (2012) 158–163.

CHAPTER SIX

Decisions when moving your mind

How does the body influence our decisions on the playing fields of sports? At first the relation between the body and sports choices seems obvious—if you get tired you simply stop running—but as you will see it is not so easy, as some get going again and others do not. I will start with decisions that are much more counterintuitive. For example, why should the body influence a judge in a gymnastics competition sitting comfortable in a chair while judging the movements of gymnasts in front of her? From the perspective of embodied choices, we would assume systematic changes in her judgments whether she is able to perform the movement she sees or cannot. If the judge observes a movement that is known by her motor system, we can assume her judgments will be more precise. How can this be tested?

In a study with one of my previous PhD students, Alexandra Pizzera, herself a gymnast, we separated gymnasts' judges into two groups. One group was able (or had been able) to perform a split-leg movement on a beam (a typical judged movement in a performance sequence on a beam), whereas the other group had no such experience. It should be noted that both groups had the same umpire license from the gymnastics professional association and had judged, on average, for the same number of years and at the same level of competition. Further, gender, age, and how often they had judged or seen competitions on TV or in a gymnastics hall were recorded to make sure that the only difference between the groups lay in the specific experience of that movement. The results were stunning. Those judges with experience in those movements judged the movements better by far than those without. How did we know? We used the rules of the Federation Internationale de Gymnastique in which the standards for technical elements in a split movement, such as leg angles, are clearly defined. For example, a leg split needs to be exactly 180 degrees. If the legs deviate between 0 and 20 degrees from 180 degrees, 0.1 point should be deducted from the final score; if more than 20-degrees deviation from 180 degrees is observed, 0.3 points should be deducted. Using video analyses of the movements and the score sheet for each gymnast, we were able to precisely measure the performance

Judgment, Decision-Making, and Embodied Choices
https://doi.org/10.1016/B978-0-12-823523-2.00006-4

of the judges. A relation between judging performance and previous motor experience in other sports led us to conclude that indeed, even judgments of other movements are influenced by one's own body. In a final study, we even trained soccer referees to foul and dive and showed that training the motor system does indeed lead to better performance [1].

Movement experience, however, needs to be quite similar to the observed action to confer an advantage. Beatriz Calvo-Merino presented capoeira and ballet dancers videos of capoeira and ballet movements while the participants were in a scanner measuring brain activity. The benefits of movement experience were experience specific. That is, capoeira dancers were good at judging capoeira movements and ballet dancers used their motor system experience to support perceptual judgments when ballet movement were shown on a screen in the scanner. Just how specific one's own experience needs to be is not fully known. In the gymnastics study mentioned earlier, judges who preferred to start the movement with their left foot were not better at judging left-foot-first gymnasts and similarly, no benefits were observed for right-footed judges observing right-footed starts.

How do we know it is not the experience of watching the movements but is actually the motor system that drives these embodied choices? One way to test this is to use experts with long-term perceptual experience but no motor experience. For example, Rouwen Canal-Bruland and colleagues tested how good participants are able to judge basketball movements. Participants are hard-core basketball fans who were in wheelchairs and compared them with athletes who had both perceptual and movement experience. The results indicated higher judgment performance when the motor system experience could be used [2]. Another way is to apply a virtual lesion to the brain using transcranial magnetic stimulation (TMS), which produces magnetic waves. In a basketball study, TMS was applied to participants' motor area when they made a perceptual judgment of whether a basketball shown in its early flight phase would end up in the basket. Results indicate that when the motor system of experts was inhibited, the perceptual judgments decreased to almost the level of novices in which the motor area was the not inhibited, indicating an important role of the motor system when making such judgments.

The findings presented earlier apply to perceptual identification, discrimination, and performance judgments. Studies have also shown that esthetic judgments are partly influenced by one's own motor system [3].

Esthetic embodied choices

I once visited Arthur Reber in New York. Arthur is the "father" of implicit learning, a way of learning that often is incidental and not even recognized by the learner as a learning process, such as learning your mother tongue by listening to others talking. Over the weekend, I had time to walk around Manhattan, and I paused for a while on a bench in Washington Square Park near New York University. Later that day, I walked to the Museum of Modern Art and saw a painting of two men sitting on a bench in Washington Square Park, just as I had. Gazing at the painting, I felt a strong connection to sitting that morning on the bench and taking in the surroundings, so strong that I went to the museum shop and bought a copy of the painting. This was not a premeditated choice; certainly it was the recent memory and the fresh bodily experiences that made me buy the picture. Even now after more than 20 years, the painting is still in my office, and when I look at it from the couch in my office it is as if I can still feel the bench in Washington Square Park.

So how are esthetic judgments made when they refer to embodied choices? Put simply, by proprioception (the sense of one's own movements or positions). Barbara Gail Montero provided a huge array of examples for why proprioception enables us to perceive esthetic qualities in others' movements or objects [4]. Relying on Emmanuel Kant, she argued that pleasure is something of an intersubjective experience on which we can disagree, but beauty is something researchers today try to quantify between subjects such as judging the beauty of faces or objects. Kant was born on April 22, 1724. Why does it matter? Well, it is interesting to me simply because I was born on April 22, some 244 years later. Sometimes, it seems that if you share something with somebody else, even a simple thing such as the date or location of your birth, your first name, or the fabric of the shirt you are wearing, it makes that person more attractive to you. Whether you like ballet because you yourself are capable of it or because you can use your proprioception to feel the dancers' grace is open to debate. For example, Montero was once a ballet dancer and thus her examples of feeling grace or overcoming gravity when observing dance movements go beyond the visual or auditory senses to explain the esthetic judgments steered by one's own proprioception. She asks, therefore, if it is possible to derive esthetic pleasure from the experience of one's own body. Her answer is yes, both from her experience as a dancer and on scientific grounds. Likewise, I argue from my own experiences and from empirical studies that yes, buying a picture and judging a gymnast can be nothing more than embodied choices. In the context of esthetic judgments, I would use the term embodied esthetic judgments that fits well with a definition of Montero: "Embodied aesthetics: One can have an aesthetic experience of one's own body as perceived through senses other than vision and audition" (p. 892) [4]. I have to admit I am not a good dancer and maybe that's why I cannot fully acknowledge the same pleasure via my proprioception when I watch ballet dancers. I do acknowledge the beauty and skill, and if I dance myself I rather enjoy being one with the music, often in my own world—so much so that my colleagues mention this at conference parties when I come back from the dance floor. I have to admit, I have no interest in seeing a video of it!

The pleasure that comes with seeing a performance, painting, or sculpture has also been called kinesthetic sympathy, motor fluency, and motor perception. Listening to Chopin, one might feel Chopin's ruthlessness [5]; viewing a sculpture [6], one might appreciate the role of touch; one might see dancelike movements in team sports [7]. Briefly, our own bodily experiences seem to influence esthetic judgments more than was previously understood. Karl-Andrew Woltin and Ana Guinote summed it up quite neatly in the title of a paper: "I can, I do and so I like: From power to action and aesthetic preferences" [8].

Sounds and embodied choices

Let us go beyond vision. Just hearing the sound of someone writing with a pencil on a piece of paper changes how you simultaneously turn circles into ellipses with your own pencil [9]. Let us get more into the world of sound and its impact on our own agency and behavior. Have you ever experienced walking in the dark and being unsure if you are hearing yourself or the footsteps of somebody following you? How do we make a judgment in this potentially scary situation? You guessed right: The motor system plays its role here, too. As we walk, we predict changes in the environment, and this includes the sounds that movements produce. When we're walking we do not pay a lot attention to these sounds, very much in contrast to when we are performing a dance-step routine [10]. So if we change our movement forces slightly and put them into a different pace, we are much better able to discriminate whether the sound was us or someone else. For schizophrenic people, this is not so easy and they often report hearing voices in their head that they think are produced from outside. It seems that the specific area in the brain responsible for this is called the temporal parietal junction (TPJ) [11]. Similarly, healthy people are not able to tickle themselves, but people with schizophrenia can [12]. Earlier, we learned about the uses of TMS. Applying it to the TPJ may change whether you attribute a presented sound to yourself or to another source. In my lab, we tested this by presenting participants in a study with their own and other sounds of hurdling movements in track and field, as these have specific rhythms we could manipulate. When healthy participants were asked to say whether a hurdling sound was theirs or someone else's, they were slightly biased toward themselves and often quite accurate. However, when we inhibited the TPJ with TMS, participants started to attribute more of the sounds to another person, replicating findings in patients with schizophrenia [13].

The acoustic information from our movements is not only used to discriminate our own effects in the environment from others; but also it is indeed quite important for us to automatically take sounds into account. On my first visit to Beijing, China, I walked from my hotel to the conference site and on several occasions I was nearly bumped into by someone on a scooter. Why was that? I figured out that in Beijing, unlike in my home country in Europe, most of the scooters were electric, and electric scooters are very quiet. Although I don't usually cross streets without looking, at home, my ears would warn me—that buzz means a scooter is coming—ahead of a decision to step into the street, before I used my eyes. In Beijing, my strategy was not of much help as e-scooters were all over the place. The same may apply to you when you are walking in Amsterdam where pedestrian and bicycle lanes are next to each other. The Amsterdamers are well known for riding their bikes fast and asserting their right to be in their lane. Now consider the recent rise of silent electric models, and woe to you if you rely solely on your ears before crossing the bike lane. The increasing number of accidents is forcing countries to enact new regulations. For examples, in the United States, manufacturers are required to equip electric cars with running sounds so that people can hear them [14]. In Melbourne, Australia, where I am writing this chapter, I have been pleased to see a sign warning bikers to make themselves noticeable when approaching pedestrians from behind on shared walking and biking lanes.

The acoustic information of our own movements (or the e-technologies that move us) can also be used to improve movements. For example, a group in Italy led by Tiziano Agostini showed that when hammer throwers in track and field sports were given acoustic feedback from their best throws they improved their throws [15]. Interestingly, making the sounds a little bit faster also produced faster movements in the next hammer throw that often led to more distance and thus better performance. In a combined study with our lab, we showed that when only specific parameters were manipulated there was no effect; rather, it was the auditory gestalt of the sounds that represented the full movement that helped improve the movement [16]. In another study, we even changed the acoustic feedback during the movement. We started with the hurdling movement as introduced earlier, as it consists of a sequence of movements, and the foot-ground contact is important for keeping a pace and rhythm. We built a little device that recorded the sound of the foot-ground contact but allowed us, unnoticed by the participants, to replay this sound exactly at the time of the contact or a little bit later [17]. What were the results? When we asked sports students to run and changed the timing of the sound, they did indeed change their movements, and with training, they improved their performance [18].

How to we predict intentions of others and generate different options to choose from?

A very important part of understanding how to make decisions in sports is learning to predict others' movements and their intentions. Consider basketball, in which deception often plays a major role and can confer an advantage to the offense. Deceiving someone with movements in basketball is not so easy, as the time between the first and the final movement needs to be quite short but still long enough that the opponent falls into the trap. Further, deceptions only work if they are not too systematic; for example, if you never use your first movement to try to deceive the defense, the defense will pick that up quite fast. How do athletes decide on their defense tactics if attackers are trying to deceive? In the lab, some research suggests that people use just a few cues and the context or situational probabilities—that is, in some situations it simply becomes more likely that one or another option will be chosen [19]. Often analyzing the gaze of defenders helps us to understand how they pick up information that allows them to anticipate a movement before it is realized. Most situations in sports are constructed in such a way that only anticipation of the opponent's movements allows the athlete to be able to respond early enough. Think about penalties and distances between the attacker and the goalkeeper and many sports with a net such as badminton, tennis, and volleyball. The same applies to an attacker's decision about what to do next. For example, we found out that experts in sports such as team handball and soccer generate options following the Take-The-First heuristic. Take-The-First assumes that if you are in a game—meaning you have limited time—you do not generate all possible options but just two or three, and then you often choose the first one you generated. If you are an expert, the first option you generate does not just randomly pop into your brain; rather, given your training you have been in many similar situations and have experienced which option in this situation is quite efficient. The Take-The-First heuristic has been shown in our lab to be a beneficial strategy in choice tasks and we argue that you should rely on your intuition (Fig. 1) [20].

These results have motivated follow-up studies, for example, with Australian football players [21], and in quite a lot of different sports or areas of application, such as medicine and navigation. We further found that not all people rely on their intuition to the same degree, and some do so more easily than others; for example, in situations in which fast choices are important, knowing how often you rely on your intuition and how often you deliberate on a problem instead of making a fast choice can help you see whether you are the right fit for the job. We tested young soccer players and showed that under time-pressure, players who could use the Take-The-First heuristic were those who had performed well. In testing over 2 years, they also improved in their performance more than those who could not rely on their intuition [22].

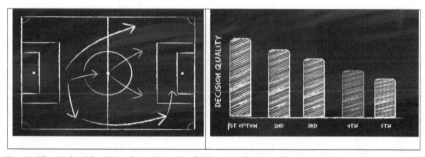

Fig. 1 The Take-The-First heuristic. (Left) Frozen frame of an attack situation in which participants are asked to generate options as the playmaker such as past to the left or right wing (*white arrows*) or to the center that has further options [*green arrows* (*gray* in print version)]. (Right) Expert players' quality of choices according to when the option is generated, most experts stop generating before the *blue bar* (*gray* in print version) and generate 2–3 options (1st, 2nd, etc.). (*Based on J.G. Johnson, M. Raab, Individual differences of action orientation for risk taking in sports. Res. Q. Exercise Sport 75 (3) (2004) 326–336; J.G. Johnson, M. Raab, Take the first: option-generation and resulting choices, Organ. Behav. Hum. Decis. Process. 91(2) (2003) 215–229.*)

I have always wished I could know what someone else was going to do just by looking into that person's eyes. This could be useful in social situations and as a practical means of predicting choices and avoiding pain. With five children, for example, I could have saved myself some heart-stopping chases if I had known one was about to run into the street. I even tried to optimize the position of cups and glasses on the dinner table, in a vain attempt to reduce the number of spilled drinks; but children's eyes do not telegraph where their arms are going to be. In my professional life, I have been somewhat more successful when using gaze behavior measured by eye-tracking cameras to predict, for example, whether a handball player is going to throw to the goal or pass to a specific teammate. Applying the ideas from the Take-The-Best heuristic, instead of the average of all fixations before they decided, I used just the first fixation on one part of the playing field. This was much better at predicting the choices than weighting and averaging all fixations [23].

Vestibular signals, touch, and embodied choices

Diane Deroualle from Marseille is interested in how vestibular signals influence our embodied choices. For example, she presented participants in a virtual reality experiment with a situation in which they were asked to toss a ball to one of the six players from the perspective of an avatar in the simulation. During the task, participants were seated on a motor-controlled chair that rotated them during the task such that their physical body on the chair was rotating in the same direction as they needed to mentally rotate to make the choice as the avatar or in the opposite direction. Participants were faster in deciding when to toss the ball to the correct player when their mental rotation was in the same direction as they were rotating in their chair [24]. Vestibular signals of the body influence our choices not only when we are rotated in a fixed place but also, for example, when we are moved passively in space. Matthias Hartmann (University of Bern) and colleagues showed that moving to the left or right when generating random numbers in a random-number generation task provides another case of an embodied choice. When moved to the left, people generated smaller numbers than when they were moved to the right. Hartmann and colleagues suggested that participants were imagining a mental number line, and the vestibular signals fired by being passively moved influenced the number they chose: Movement to the left-generated numbers toward the left end of the line

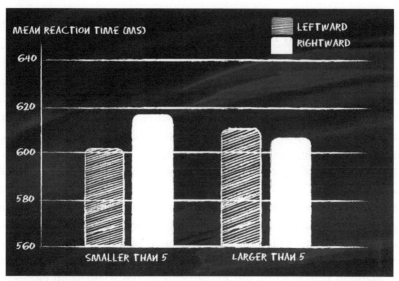

Fig. 2 Mean reaction time (ms) for large numbers (>5) and small numbers (<5) during whole-body motion (leftward vs rightward).

(i.e., smaller numbers) and movement to the right-generated larger numbers (Fig. 2) [25].

Earlier, I discussed that grasping at an object and grasping an idea are actually bound together in development. Even simple mental rotation performance has been found to be related to infants' motor development [26]. Sigmund Freud and later many other developmental psychologists realized that touching objects produces a better understanding of them. But is touch in learning scientific facts beneficial?

Zacharias Zacharia (University of Cyprus) reviewed a number of studies that focused on embodied choices and science experimentation in school. He also conducted a number of studies himself on whether touching objects provides better outcomes in learning about, for example, testing learning when students measuring mass with a triple beam balance, free fall, electric circuits, pendulum movement, and temperature in physics. In 13 studies involving students from the age of 5 years to young adult, he found that touching helped people learn physical laws. In contrast to control groups that were not allowed to use haptic (i.e., based on touch) feedback to learn, participants who were allowed to touch performed better on tests of their knowledge [27].

Movement in high-stakes decisions

When movements are part of high-stakes decisions the movements change as well as the decisions. Have you ever scrambled up a tree, hiked a trail through the woods, or climbed a mountain? Emotions certainly played a role when you were engaged in those activities, and indeed, emotions have often been said to play a role in action preparedness: I am sure you have heard, for example, the phrase "fight or flight." In lab research, one way to study the role of emotions has been through climbing [28]. For example, Raoul Oudejans (Vrije University, Amsterdam) found that when climbers were tasked with reaching higher heights, gaze analyses revealed they assessed more distant but reachable holds but ended up grasping the closer holds just to be safe. Using the Trier Social Stress test, my colleagues and I have shown that in stressful situations, such as making high-stake decisions, our attention is focused on our movements, as this is our main interaction with the world [29]. In the Trier Social Stress test, subjects must perform while being observed by white-coated experts. The test is used quite often to induce stress. Cortisol (the stress hormone) and behavioral changes are often measured to see the effects of such stress manipulations; changes in focus or movements are also indications that the body indeed plays a role in making embodied choices.

Replicating in the lab the kind of real-world stress that one would experience, say, in a FIFA World Cup final is not always easy, but you may remember hearing about the Milgram experiment of the 1960s, in which experimenters put people under extreme stress by convincing them that they were applying real electric shocks (at least that was what the participants believed) to a victim in a learning experiment. I recall very vividly how the coach team in a second league volleyball team discussed how to increase competitional stress in training. We considered setting up situations in which at the end of a game each point would really matter—if a player was not making points we, for example, would increase the number of hours of training that evening by literally closing the door. Another idea that did not really help the team's atmosphere and performance was that all players would need to perform an extra strength skill after a failure—except, that is, for the one who made the mistake. He would have to sit out and watch the others suffer. We were players in peak condition and we did not make mistakes because we did not care but rather simply because we were tired at the end of a game or happened to make a small error, as everyone did from time to time. Performance was actually better when we were motivated by our own and the team's success, so later we gave up on some of the group punishments that seemed to have little success in preparing us to make high-stakes decisions. Similarly, in experiments we tried a similar kind of pressure, such as showing participants pictures of poor children in Africa to whom we would donate money, but only if the participants hit a target. This manipulation worked as a stressor, inducing changes in hitting performance, but not in the desired direction: Performance decreased in this condition, and even training could not easily get our participants to improve beyond their base rate performance. Full disclosure: These experiments were approved by the local ethics commission because we actually donated all the money later, independent of whether they hit or missed the target, and we explained to our subjects that we needed to deceive them to test them in such stressful situations.

References

[1] A. Pizzera, M. Raab, Does motor or visual experience enhance the detection of deceptive movements in football? Int. J. Sports Sci. Coach. 7 (2) (2012) 269–283.

[2] P.G. Renden, S. Kerstens, R.R.D. Oudejans, R. Cañal-Bruland, Foul or dive? Motor contributions to judging ambiguous foul situations in football. Eur. J. Sport Sci. 14 (Sup. 1) (2012) S221–S227, https://doi.org/10.1080/17461391.2012.683813.

[3] B. Calvo-Merino, J. Grezes, D.E. Glaser, R.E. Passingham, P. Haggard, Seeing or doing? Influence of visual and motor familiarity in action observation, Curr. Biol. 16 (19) (2006) 1905–1910.

[4] Barbara Gail Montero on embodied aesthetics inA. Newen, L. De Bruin, S. Gallagher (Eds.), The Oxford Handbook of 4E Cognition, Oxford Press, Oxford, UK, 2018, pp. 891–910.

[5] C. Rosen, Piano Notes: The World of the Pianist, Free Press, New York, 2002.

[6] R. Zuckert, Sculpture and touch: Herder's aesthetics of sculptures, J. Aesthet. Art Critic. 67 (3) (2009) 285–299.

[7] T. Cohen, Sports and art: beginning questions, in: J. Andre, D.N. James (Eds.), Rethinking Colleague Athletes, Temple University Press, Philadelphia, 1991, pp. 298–304.

[8] K.A. Woltin, A. Guinote, I can, I do, and so I like: from power to action and aesthetic preferences. J. Exp. Psychol. Gen. (2015). https://doi.org/10.1037/xge0000095.

[9] E. Thoret, M. Aramaki, L. Bringeeoux, S. Ystad, R. Kronland-Mertinet, Seeing circles and drawing ellipses: when sound biases reproduction of visual motion, PLoS One 11 (4) (2016) e0154475.

[10] N. Heins, J. Pomp, D.S. Kluger, I. Trempler, K. Zentgraf, M. Raab, R.I. Schubotz, Incidental orIntentional? Different brain responses to one's own action sounds in hurdling vs. tap dancing, Front. Neurosci. 14 (2020) 483.

[11] N. Dougall, N. Maayan, K. Soares-Weiser, L.M. McDermott, A. McIntosh, Transcranial magnetic stimulation (TMS) for schizophrenia. Cochrane Database Syst. Rev. 8 (2015). https://doi.org/10.1002/14651858.CD006081.pub2 Art. No.: CD006081.

[12] S.J. Blakemore, D. Wolpert, C. Frith, Why can't you tickle yourself? Neuroreport 11 (11) (2000) R11–R16.

[13] C. Justen, C. Herbert, K. Werner, M. Raab, Self vs. other: neural correlates underlying agent identification based on unimodal auditory information as revealed by electro-tomography (sLORETA). Neuroscience 259 (2014) 25–34, https://doi.org/10.1016/j.neuroscience.2013.11.042.

[14] https://en.wikipedia.org/wiki/Electric_vehicle_warning_sounds.

[15] T. Agostini, G. Righi, A. Galmonte, P. Bruno, The relevance of auditory information in optimizing hammer throwers performance, in: B. Pascolo (Ed.), Biomechanics and Sports, Springer, Vienna, 2004, pp. 67–74.

[16] M. Murgia, T. Hohmann, A. Galmonte, M. Raab, T. Agostini, Recognising one's own motor actions through sound: the role of temporal factors. Perception 41 (8) (2012) 976–987, https://doi.org/10.1068/p7227.

[17] C. Kennel, T. Hohmann, M. Raab, Action perception via auditory information: agent identification and discrimination with complex movement sounds. J. Cogn. Psy-chother. 26 (2) (2014) 157–165, https://doi.org/10.1080/20445911.2013.869226; C. Kennel, A. Pizzera, T. Hohmann, R.I. Schubotz, M. Murgia, T. Agostini, M. Raab, The perception of natural and modulated movement sounds. Perception 43 (8) (2014) 796–804, https://doi.org/10.1068/p7643.

[18] A. Pizzera, T. Hohmann, L. Streese, A. Habbig, M. Raab, Long-term effects of acoustic reafference training (ART). Eur. J. Sport Sci. 17 (10) (2017) 1279–1288, https://doi.org/10.1080/17461391.2017.1381767.

[19] R.C. Jackson, R. Cañal-Bruland, Deception in sport, in: A.M. Williams, R.C. Jackson (Eds.), Anticipation and Decision Making in Sport, Routledge, Abingdon, Oxon, 2019, pp. 99–116.

[20] J.G. Johnson, M. Raab, Take the first: option-generation and resulting choices, Organ. Behav. Hum. Decis. Process. 91 (2) (2003) 215–229.

[21] T. Buszard, D. Farrow, J. Kemp, Examining the influence of acute instructional approaches on the decision-making performance of experienced team field sport players. J. Sports Sci. 31 (3) (2013) 238–247, https://doi.org/10.1080/02640414.2012.731516.

[22] L. Musculus, R. Azzurra, M. Raab, B.H. Lobinger, A developmental perspective on option generation and selection. Dev. Psychol. (2018). https://doi.org/10.1037/dev0000665.

[23] A. Glöckner, T. Heinen, J.G. Johnson, M. Raab, Network approaches for expert deci-sions in sports, Hum. Mov. Sci. 31 (2012) 318–333; M. Raab, J.G. Johnson, Expertise-based differences in search and option-generation strategies. J. Exp. Psychol. Appl. 13 (3) (2007) 158–170, https://doi.org/10.1037/1076-898X.13.3.158.

[24] D. Deroualle, et al., Changing perspective: the role of vestibular signals, Neuropsychologica 79 (2015) 175–183.

[25] M. Hartmann, L. Grabherr, F.W. Mast, Moving along the mental number line, J. Exp. Psychol. Hum. Percept. Perform. 38 (6) (2012) 1416–1427.

[26] W. Möhring, A. Frick, Touching up mental rotation: effects of manual experience on 6-month-old infants' mental object rotation. Child Dev. 84 (2013) 1554–1565, https://doi.org/10.1111/cdev.12065.

[27] Z. Zacharia, Examining whether touch sensory feedback is necessary for science learning through experimentation: a literature review of two different lines of research across K-16. Educ. Res. Rev. 16 (2015) 116–137, https://doi.org/10.1016/j.edurev.2015.10.001.

[28] J.R. Pijpers, R.R.D. Oudejans, F.C. Bakker, Anxiety-induced changes in movement behaviour during the execution of a complex whole-body task, Q. J. Exp. Psychol. 58A (2005) 421–445.

[29] F. Lautenbach, S.J.P. Laborde, P. Putman, A. Angelidis, M. Raab, Attentional distrac-tion by negative sports words in athletes under low- and high-pressure conditions: evi-dence from the sport emotional Stroop task. Sport Exerc. Perform. Psychol. 5 (4) (2016) 296–307, https://doi.org/10.1037/spy0000073.

CHAPTER SEVEN

Embodied choices in real life

In the last chapters, I focused on the empirical evidence showing that the body is actually more involved in our choices than previously thought. However, most of the evidence comes from very controlled lab experiments and it is not clear how much the results generalize to real-life situations. Therefore it makes sense to describe some of the findings that at least the authors of the papers have argued are applicable to real life. Often the choices considered are those made in the domains of medicine, shopping, and finance, among many others that most people find important in their own lives.

Medical decisions

Medical decisions are certainly of personal interest to everybody. And yes, research on decision-making in this area is impressive. But how is the body involved in a doctor's decision-making? Here, not so much is known. For example, you remember Danzinger's study on judges that indicated different decision thresholds before or after lunch. To the best of my knowledge, no one has yet conducted this experiment with doctors. However, it is well established that decisions can be influenced by a person's current physical and mental fatigue, and you may prefer a doctor who has just arrived for work than one at the end of a 24- or even 48-h shift [1]. There are also quite a number of reports that during night shifts, nurses have had the feeling that something was not quite right with a patient, even though the data looked good. Often these intuitions have been correct, adding to the evidence that spontaneous thoughts are meaningful and often accurate [2]. If you ask people how much insight a thought can display, rated by its degree of spontaneity, it seems that the more fluently a thought is produced, the more people believe in its quality. For example, intuitions, dreaming, and Freudian slips are often believed to have higher value in contrast to rumination, deliberation, or logic [3]. One reason, as discussed earlier, is that the body has a system that actually produces these gut feelings if we allow it. Consider another example from the medical domain: coronary care unit (CCU) decisions. In emergency rooms, doctors routinely have to decide whether to send a patient with chest pain to the CCU or a regular nursing bed. Doctors facing this decision in one Michigan hospital relied on defensive decision-making—that is, they protected themselves against potential lawsuits—and sent about 90% of the patients to the CCU even though only about 25% of them actually had a coronary problem that warranted being sent there [4]. As a consequence, the unit became overcrowded, the quality of care declined, and medical costs increased. One attempted solution was to provide doctors with the Heart Disease Predictive Instrument (HDPI), a chart with some 50 probabilities and a pocket calculator with a logistic regression function to determine the probability that the patient needed to be sent to the CCU. The HDPI made better allocations than physicians' defensive decision-making, but physicians disliked using a tool that they did not understand.

Inspired by the Take-The-Best heuristic, Lee Green and David Mehr from the University of Michigan developed and implemented a fast-and-frugal decision tree to replace the HDPI. The tree asks three questions only: (1) Is there a certain anomaly (ST-segment changes) in the electrocardiogram? (2) Is chest pain the chief complaint? and (3) Are there are any other factors present such as myocardial infarction or nitroglycerin use for chest pain relief? Unlike a full decision tree with n^2 exits ($n=$ number of questions), a fast-and-frugal tree has $n+1$ exits, with one exit at each question and two at the final question. Thus it allows decisions to be made faster and with limited information and is intuitively understandable (intuitive design). But how accurate is it? A study at the hospital reported that it led to fewer misses and a better false-alarm rate than both the HDPI and physicians' unaided decisions, the latter being even slightly below chance. The fast-and-frugal tree is still used by the physicians, who can easily adapt it to new patient populations because they understand its structure [5]. A fast-and-frugal tree in this case, for example, asked a list of questions such as irregular heartbeats, chief complaint of chest pain and at any level of such a tree, a decision can be made for coronary care unit or regular care unit based on a few but important cues. Often such decisions are based on the intuition of person's behavior and previous cases that are not fully conscious and thus gut feeling inform such choices. This strategy of providing doctors with a tool that allows them to rely on their intuition and that focuses on a few but important signals uses their own gut feelings to make more accurate decisions than a complex computer-based tool.

Communicating with patients is a very important skill for doctors. Often doctors themselves have to remember how to do a calculation or get the numbers right when asked to interpret conditional probabilities. Research indicates that doctors often ignore the base rate of an illness, which has been termed the base-rate fallacy. Gerd Gigerenzer showed that providing natural frequencies instead of conditional probabilities allowed doctors, patients, and indeed most people to understand much more easily. Paul Griffiths and Karola Stotz pinpointed this in the following example:

> Suppose your insurance company requires you to take an HIV test, which turns out positive. Your doctor informs you that there is a 0.01% chance that the result is a false positive and you are, in fact, not infected. He also tells you that the prevalence of HIV infection within the group to which you belong (female, heterosexual, no known risk) is also 0.01%. Are you comforted?

Most people, as tests have shown, are not. The critical base rate data are apparently ignored. The situation changes when the same information is given in natural frequencies: One woman in 10,000 is expected to have the virus, and her test will be positive. Of the remaining 9999 women who have done the test but do not have the virus, one will also get a positive result. With this information you can easily see that despite your positive result there is a 1 in 2 chance that you do not have HIV. Gigerenzer claimed that under the conditions in which your statistical reasoning abilities evolved, statistical information would accumulate in the form of natural frequencies. Rather than learning that a rustle in the bushes has a 0.01% false positive rate and that the base rate of rabbits in bushes is 0.01%, you would have learned that every second rustle in the bushes is a false alarm [6]. Later, when I discuss real-life decisions I will provide more examples of how using natural frequencies can inform better decisions in the field of medicine, for examples, with simple fact boxes.

Shopping decisions

In the Netherlands, a research group observed people shopping in supermarkets either holding a basket in the crook of their elbow (i.e., in a flexed position) or pushing a shopping cart with both arms in an extended position. Those that had the flexed (i.e., approach) arm position bought more candy from in front of the cashier than those who had the extended (i.e., avoidance) arm position (Fig. 1) [7].

Consumer choice, a research area that tries to understand how people choose food or other consumables, has used embodied cognition as a framework as well. For example, in one study [8], consumers reported making

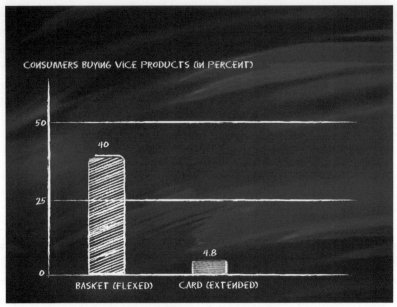

Fig. 1 Carrying a basket (arm in flexed position) versus pushing a cart (arms in extended position) influences the likelihood of purchasing candy.

impulse purchases and verbalized that specific items "stood out from the rest," a feeling that would not go away until the item was purchased [9]. I would go even further and would say that such embodied choices are partly due to routine behavior biased by previous encounters and advertisements and partly to gut feelings.

Liking people

Liking people often starts with a first impression. A gut feeling may provide you with a short emotional reaction when meeting people. Sometimes a first impression can be overruled following multiple encounters, but if you are in the business of hiring or choosing people, trusting your first impression is a fundamental skill. However, predicting how a future student or employee will perform in the coming years is not an easy task, and deciding between multiple candidates is not an easy choice [10].

Elections provide another example of the role of gut feelings in liking people. Voters often simply rely on a few impressions gleaned from media coverage of candidates' campaigns and use only a few but valid cues [11]. Interestingly the hand that presidential candidates use to gesture with in their talks seems to matter, and whether it matches the observer's dominant hand [12]. As discussed earlier, gestures with the right and left hand may reflect preferences and attributions of good (right) or bad (left) in cultures that often have 20% left handers and a cultural heritage that produces such associations. The first impression in a job interview can sometime overshadow measures of performance that are often quite predictive and quantifiable, such as the cognitive performance on the Graduate Record Examination, used in graduate school admissions decisions in the United States [13].

Sometimes these first impressions need to be fast and are not about liking but about assessing threat or potential risk, such as when law enforcement officers respond to a call or an airport security agent suspects smuggling [14]. When emotional judgments of others need to be made, we use our own motor system. For example, when transcranial magnetic stimulation was applied to participants to inhibit the right primary motor cortex and somatosensory cortices, they were no longer good at detecting changes in facial expressions of others [15]. However, these effects were found only in females and have been interpreted as females being more active in embodied mimicry to enhance emotion understanding. Differences in mimicry have also been shown in other nonverbal behavior; for example, when women nod to their communication partner it reflects that they are listening, whereas men nod only if in agreement with the argument. Being in a social environment sometimes means someone is socially rejected. A video game in which participants pass a ball to each other has been used to explore whether social rejection can be induced in a virtual game. Researchers found that if they manipulated the game such that one of the participants did not receive the ball, social rejection could be effected. In a study that may need further replication, this social rejection produced a reduction of skin temperature, another direct effect of embodied cognition and its consequences for embodied choices [16]. Skin is not acknowledged much in embodied choices and I think this is a mistake. If you have time to read the book "embodied minds" from Jay Seitz published 2019, in Chapter 2 about the significance of the skin you will find a huge amount of argument why we should consider the skin more in embodied research [17].

Liking objects

Esthetic choices are a research area in themselves [18]. Unlike many of the embodied choices I described earlier, esthetic choices are about preferences, not inferences. For example, whether you like an object, say a painting, is based on your preferences and cannot be measured as right or wrong. I guess that why we use gut feelings indicating that personal preferences are connected to your feelings.

Gut feelings certainly play more of a role in judgments that refer to preferences (what a person likes) than to inferences (what is a correct answer). Interestingly, embodied choices play a role here. Consider being offered a free poster as a student on a campus. Would it matter whether you were randomly assigned to one, chose one within seconds, or had time to choose deliberatively (Fig. 2)?

Later, the experimenter asked those students who received a free poster if they would be willing to sell the poster that they chose. Guess what—those who were randomly assigned a poster were willing to sell it for much less (about 4 dollars) than those who chose intuitively or deliberatively (about 6 dollars) [19].

Often choosing something with your gut makes you like it even more and you more strongly want to keep it, as A.P. Dijksterhuis (University of Amsterdam, Netherlands) has demonstrated for quite a number of preference choices, from posters to apartments [20]. How do we get into these unconscious thought situations in which the body may signal information for better choices? A.P. Dijksterhuis asked people to do a second task to distract them from consciously thinking about the primary task, such as

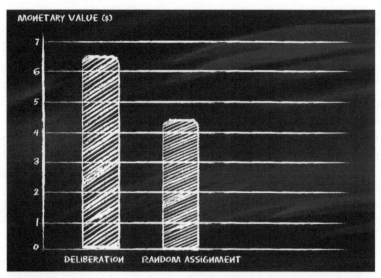

Fig. 2 Monetary value given to a poster depended on whether participants were assigned to a deliberation or random condition.

choosing an apartment or poster. A typical task for this purpose is an n-back task, where n refers to the number of trials in the task. In an n-back task, participants see stimuli appear sequentially on the screen. They have to store the stimuli in their working memory, as they are then asked to indicate when the current stimulus matches the one from n trials previous (the higher n is, the more difficult the task). Another way that is not as active is to give people a task involving future decision making and to probe them once in a while about what they are thinking. Studies have indicated that this probing reveals how much people's minds wander in these situations, as opposed to consciously performing the task. Jonathon Smallwood (Max Planck Institute for Human Cognitive and Brain Sciences, Leipzig, Germany) and colleagues found in delay discounting that mind wandering is beneficial to solving a task [21]. After completing an easy and a difficult attention task, participants were asked to choose between a smaller reward immediately or a larger one in 180 days. Participants whose mind wandered more in the easy task that allowed for mind wandering chose the latter and larger reward more often than those whose mind wandered less in that task. The results were interpreted as showing that the mind wandering was related to the future and what potentially could be done with the larger reward, and thus again the body may have played its role here. The authors argued that tasks that allow for mindfulness, a strategy of listening to your current state and thus listening to your own gut feelings, may have produced such effects.

References

[1] G.P. Krueger, Sustained work, fatigue, sleep loss and performance: a review of the issues. Work Stress. 3 (2) (1989) 129–141, https://doi.org/10.1080/02678378908256939; J. Horne, Working throughout the night: beyond 'sleepiness'—impairments to critical decision making, Neurosci. Biobehav. Rev. 36 (10) (2012) 2226–2231.

[2] J. Fedo, Nurses' Decision Making and Pain Management Outcomes. 321, (Doctoral dissertations) https://opencommons.uconn.edu/dissertations/321, 2014.

[3] SeeC.K. Morewedge, D. Kupor, When the absence of reasoning breeds meaning: metacognitive appraisals of spontaneous thought, in: K.C.E. Fox, K. Christoff (Eds.), The Oxford Handbook of Spontaneous Thought, Oxford University Press, Oxford, UK, 2018, pp. 35–46.

[4] L.A. Green, D.R. Mehr, What alters physicians' decisions to admit to the coronary care unit? J. Fam. Pract. 45 (1997) 219–226.

[5] O. Wegwarth, W. Gaissmaier, G. Gigerenzer, Smart strategies for doctors and doctors-in-training: heuristics in medicine. Med. Educ. 43 (2009) 721–728, https://doi.org/10.1111/j.1365-2923.2009.03359.x.

[6] P. Griffiths, K. Stotz, How the mind grows: a developmental perspective on the biology of cognition, Synthese 122 (2000) 29–51.

[7] B. van Den Bergh, J. Schmitt, L. Warlop, Embodied myopia. J. Market. Res. 48 (6) (2011) 1033–1044, https://doi.org/10.1509/jmr.09.0503.

[8] D.W. Rook, The buying impulse, J. Consum. Res. 14 (September) (1987) 189–199.

[9] See more examples inA.J. Malter, An introduction to embodied cognition: implications for consumer research, in: K.P. Corfman, J.G. Lynch Jr. (Eds.), Advances in Consumer Research, vol. 23, Association for Consumer Research, Provo, UT, 1996, pp. 272–276.

[10] D.S. Chapman, K.L. Uggerslev, S.A. Carroll, K.A. Piasentin, D.A. Jones, Applicant attraction to organizations and job choice: a meta-analytic review of the correlates of recruiting outcomes, J. Appl. Psychol. 90 (2005) 928–944.

[11] A. Graefe, J.S. Armstrong, Predicting elections from the most important issue: a test of the take-the-best heuristic, J. Behav. Decis. Mak. 25 (1) (2012) 41–48.

[12] D. Casasanto, K. Jasmin, Good and bad in the hands of politicians: spontaneous gestures during positive and negative speech. PLoS One 5 (7) (2010) e11805, https://doi.org/10.1371/journal.pone.0011805.

[13] R.M. Dawes, The robust beauty of improper linear models of decision making, Am. Psychol. 34 (1979) 571–582.

[14] T. Pachur, G. Marinello, Expert intuitions: how to model the decision strategies of airport customs officers? Acta Psychol. 144 (1) (2013) 97–103.

[15] S. Korb, J. Malsert, V. Rochas, T.A. Rihs, S.W. Rieger, S. Schwab, et al., Gender differences in the neural network of facial mimicry of smiles—an rTMS study, Cortex 70 (2015) 101–114.

[16] H. IJzerman, M. Gallucci, W.T.J.L. Pouw, S.C. Weißgerber, N.J. Van Doesum, K.D. Williams, Cold-blooded loneliness: social exclusion leads to lower skin temperatures. Acta Psychol. 140 (3) (2012) 283–288, https://doi.org/10.1016/j.actpsy.2012.05.002.

[17] J. Seitz, Embodied Minds, Peter Land Publisher, New York, NY, 2019.

[18] J. Levinson (Ed.), The Oxford Handbook of Aesthetics, Oxford University Press, Oxford, UK, 2003.

[19] C.E. Gilblin, C.K. Morewedge, M.I. Norton, Unexpected benefits of deciding by mind wandering, Front. Psychol. 4 (2013) 598.

[20] A.P. Dijksterhuis, W. Maarten, L.F. Bos, R.B. Nordgren, B. Rick, R.B. Van Baaren, On making the right choice: the deliberation-without-attention effect, Science 17 (2006) 1005–1007.

[21] J. Smallwood, F.J.M. Ruby, T. Singer, Letting go of the present: mind-wandering is associated with reduced delay discounting, Conscious. Cogn. 22 (2013) 1–7.

CHAPTER EIGHT

Individual and cultural differences in embodied choices

"To understand" in the German language is *begreifen*, which stems from the word *greifen*, meaning to grasp. To say one grasps an idea appears in other languages too, and goes back to the idea that to understand something you need to act upon it. Children naturally touch everything to learn about their world and adults later use these experiences to prepare actions involving objects known to be, say, slippery, heavy, or sharp. These learned actions are further used in tasks in which neither touch nor actions are required. For example, imagine you are sitting in front of a computer screen and are given a problem-solving task such as this one: You see glasses, and each has the exact capacity of water it can contain (in milliliters) written above the glass. You also see an empty glass that should be filled to its stated capacity using any combination of the three glasses. This task is called the water jar problem, and it is solved mathematically, by some combination of adding, subtracting, and multiplying (e.g., filling up the first glass on the left 2 times with the amount in the third glass will solve the problem $168\,\text{mL} + (2 \times 277\,\text{mL}) = 722\,\text{mL}$, Can you find a solution using subtraction as well? (Fig. 1).

In a laboratory experiment with this task, participants were told in a cover story that they would be asked to repeat the task with breaks in between. In the breaks between trials, participants were asked to move their arms so that researchers could measure and understand whether active breaks help boost problem-solving performance. Unbeknownst to the participants, the movements they performed were identical in their movement trajectories but had two different functions that should activate concepts of putting something together, as in addition, or taking something away, as in subtraction. To do this, we used three bowls in which the participants moved marbles either from the outer bowls to the middle bowl, activating addition, or from the middle bowl to the outer bowls, activating subtraction. The results show that activating the specific concept of, say, addition produces more water jar problem solutions that add glasses, whereas activating the concept of subtraction produces more solutions that divide volumes of water [1]. It seems that motor control and motor feedback help adults to solve problems,

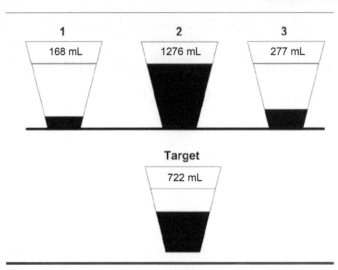

Fig. 1 Water-jar problem. *(From K. Werner, M. Raab, Moving hands, Psychol. Res. (2016) 5. Used with permission from Exp. Psychol. 60 (6) (2013) 403–409. © 2013 Hogrefe Publishing, www.hogrefe.com, https://doi.org/10.1027/1618-3169/a000213).*

and studies have shown that movement feedback is even more important for children solving such tasks. Those who are allowed to use their hands in the water jar problem perform better than those who are not [2]. And it is not just hand movements—other studies have shown that you can produce the same effects by moving your eyes [3]. You remember when we discussed the mental number line that people often relate right with higher and left with lower numbers. Well, moving to the left or right or moving forward or backward produces the same effects [4]. Whether I move you in space or you move yourself in space, it seems that you automatically activate the concepts of future and past or higher and lower numbers. If I ask you to generate random numbers, we simply assume that you will generate larger numbers when moving to the right in Western societies, as the mental number line goes from small numbers on the left to large numbers on the right, and the reverse for those cultures that read from right to left [5]. This is an indication that our early movement experiences such as reading direction and attentional allocation influence even simple things such as randomly generating numbers. What I want to emphasize is that all these culturally based experiences, learned or given, such as gender or being left-handed, are driving factors in the choices we make. This aspect of decision making has been under-acknowledged but is given an existence proof in the studies cited in this book.

Do women and left-handers have better intuition?

As mentioned earlier, left-handers gesture differently, and in some cultures, being left-handed is perceived as wrong or bad. We also saw that at the same time, left-handers have an advantage in certain sports. So, is there any advantage for embodied choices to being left-handed? Being a lefty myself, this is something I've thought about. Outside of sports I have most often seen a disadvantage, given the environment is often structured for the majority, that is, for right-handers. Consider the arrangement of desks in schools in relation to windows, as well as scissors and other tools. A day in a left-hander shop in Los Angeles was heaven for me. Whatever I touched simply fit my preferred action orientation, so much so that I bought a lefty potato peeler.

In sports, however, the advantage may not be just that an opponent may have less experience with left-handers' movements and thus have a harder time anticipating the left-hander's actions. A neuroscientific study has also shown that being strictly left-handed and having a strong right sighting-eye produces right hemispheric control of the dominant hand and visuospatial attention processing that seems to be advantageous [6]. Writing this as a left-hander, I may be biased about the benefits of being a lefty, but it is clear that asymmetrically biased attention or the existence of dominant eyes, arms, or legs supports the idea of embodied choices. Throughout evolutionary history, if a person was falling out of a tree there was no time to think on the way down which arm to use to find a hold. Dominance in the system makes the choice simple and embodied. In modern societies, it seems we are almost forced to type with both hands on keyboards or shoot to the goal in soccer with either the left or right foot, whatever our laterality preferences are.

Nevertheless, asking questions such as how embodied choices are made when genes define what you are given primes similar questions, such as, whether women are more intuitive or rely more heavily on their gut decisions. If you ask such questions in public you might hear a number of opinions. And science partly reflects this, as well. For example, research on nonverbal communication skill has clearly shown that on average, women read facial expressions of emotions better than their male counterparts. How this skill is used in embodied choices is still an open question, but one thing that is known is that these intuitions themselves can produce positive emotions and that providing emotional cues can produce more intuitive decisions and can boost confidence in one's choices [7]. It seems that on average, women do have a slight advantage here but most of the large self-report studies have relied on questionnaires that mirror society-specific expectations, and this influenced the answers; that is, participants were influenced by their own society's norms. Until, we know more about how age, gender, handedness, and other factors influence embodied choices, it makes sense to trust your intuition when you are confronted with a situation your bodily experience of previous situations can be transferred to. We are now just beginning to understand how gut feelings actually do much of the work of making choices.

Embodied higher cognitive functions

In a series of experiments, Angela Leung (School of Social Sciences, Singapore) and colleagues tested whether a metaphor I assume you are familiar with—"thinking outside the box"—can be literally and spatially used to inhibit or increase creativity. In one of their studies, 102 undergraduates completed a 10-item remote associate test (RAT), which measures thinking performance by producing a fourth word (e.g., tape) that can be associated with three target words (e.g., measure, worm, and video). The important manipulation is that one-third of the students were sitting in a 5' by 5' box, the next one-third outside of this box, and the remaining one-third (controls) in an average-sized room. The findings suggest that performing the RAT "outside the box" produced better performance compared with the two other conditions (Fig. 2). These experimental results and similar results for other creativity metaphors can be seen as a demonstration of embodied choices.

Consider a stronger manipulation of movements to enhance creativity. Michael Slepian from Tufts University and Nalini Ambady from Stanford University asked participants to follow drawings with either fluid and curved movements or nonfluid movements with a lot of sharp turns. The results of three experiments show that fluid arm movements led to enhanced creativity in the RAT, to enhanced creative generation such as generating as many creative uses of a newspaper as possible within 1 minute, and finally to enhanced cognitive flexibility; for example, flexible thinkers are more likely to include camel in the category vehicle [8].

If creativity can be boosted by movements, why do we not more often "walk and talk" when something needs to be new and innovative? Well, in academia, some people do walk and talk. For example, in the yearly retreats

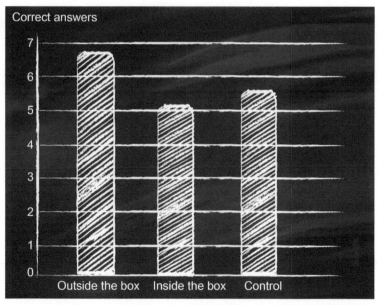

Fig. 2 Correct answers in the remote associate test for participants sitting outside the box, inside the box, or in a control condition.

of our research team in Performance Psychology, some of the day program involves questions to be discussed when walking in small groups. Here, importantly, most of the group believes in the positive effect of exercise on cognition, and thus it is unclear whether the effect is actually due to higher motivation to self-fulfill the belief or to the body somehow driving the creative process. Experiments that control many alternative explanations can circumvent this problem. Consider the work of Marily Oppezzo and Daniel L. Schwartz at Stanford University. In four experiments they systematically compared the influences of sitting and walking on creativity during and shortly after an intervention. The authors used the Guilford alternate uses test of creative divergent thinking in which participants are simply asked to generate as many possible ideas for what can be done with a brick or a second thumb on each of our hands. Eighty-one percent of participants increased their creativity scores after walking. Further, they showed that the effect was stable for other creativity measures as well. Notably, pushing people in a wheelchair did not produce the same effect as walking alone (Fig. 3) [9].

This research received much media attention [10], and thus it is not surprising that Mark Zuckerberg, cofounder and CEO of Facebook, was

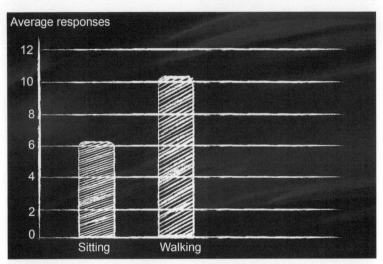

Fig. 3 Average number of responses (i.e., novel uses of an object) on Guilford's alternate uses test, showing the effects of walking versus sitting on divergent thinking.

spotted holding meetings as walks in the woods. Steve Jobs, the late cofounder of Apple, was also known for his "walking meetings." In his biography *Steve Jobs*, Walter Isaacson recalled Jobs insisting that their meetings take place on foot. Research and self-reports seem to confirm the benefits of movement, and controlled experiments are being designed to try to understand why and when creativity can be boosted by movements. Studies are not limited to walking or push-and-pull arm movements, and journals such as the *Creativity Research Journal* are full of many examples. My current favorite is from 2015 by JongHan Kim, showing how creativity is improved by squeezing a soft but not a hard ball [11].

The relation of embodied choices to self-control is also very interesting. As argued earlier, we do not always run our lives on autopilot with the body as the driver. Rather, we often reflect on the current situation and use top-down processes to influence our current situation. Consider self-control in its relation to the body and embodied choices. Often, we are confronted with desires that can keep us busy for up to 20% of our waking time, such as our urges for food, distraction, sports, sex, and sleep, among many more. Wilhelm Hofmann and colleagues [12] from Cologne, Germany, showed that when participants were contacted at random times, half of them reported thinking about acting on such desires and 42% reported resisting, using self-control. It seems that our self-control has its limits, which is also true for our bodily system: What the body needs is not endlessly available (e.g., the nutrients our muscles need to run a marathon). It seems the body can be quite easily used to influence the willpower to resist, for example, when people in the lab were asked to put their hands into ice water or to resist eating chocolate chip cookies, their choices changed. Research shows that submerging a hand in ice water or to resist eating cookies increased impulse spending, aggression, and the tendency to engage in inappropriate sexual behavior and drive when drinking [13].

From what I described earlier, the body seems to be quite involved, and thus the concept of embodied choices seems to be valid when describing how we behave. I also argued that we can resist bodily desires. Of course, willpower and self-control studies show that our choices are often influenced by a mixture of many factors within nature and nurture. One general higher cognitive factor that may affect how embodied choices are realized is personality. Earlier I illustrated this with a discussion of personality traits and the preferences for how you process information. Another important area is intelligence, as it allows different individuals to use and process information differently and thus produces potentially different embodied choices. As Thomas H. Huxley (1825–95) said, "The great end of life is not knowledge but action," and Gerd Gigerenzer and I have argued that the use of smart but simple heuristics may be a different description of intelligence from what is currently measured in intelligence tests and reflected in IQ scores [14].

Finally, let us focus on problem-solving. In problem-solving, in contrast to creativity tasks, one or more solutions can be judged as correct, such as in the Rubik's cube each side of the cube is filled with one color and there are more than one way to get there. Or consider the Tower of Hanoi (also known as the Tower of London) game, you find three pillars on a wooden desk. Three (or more) disks of different sizes are placed on the left pillar such that the largest disk is at the bottom, the middle-size disk in the middle, and the smallest disk on top. The task is to move the disks to the right pillar by moving only one disk at each turn and such that a larger disk never sits on a smaller one. If you want to try this yourself, there are numerous animations and solutions for different numbers of disks online, and links can be found on Wikipedia [15]. In an interesting study, researchers in Taiwan provided a group of students with variants of the Tower of London problem after a moderate to vigorous aerobic exercise. This exercise group's performance on the Tower of London was compared with that of a control group. The exercise group performed 30 min of exercise on a stationary bicycle at moderate to vigorous intensity, whereas the control group read for

30 min. Students in the exercise group showed better planning and problem-solving. This may have been partly the result of higher attention and alertness, or as the authors argued, the exercise may have had a facilitative effect on the executive functions of planning and problem-solving, indicating that these are embodied choices [16].

Most of the results supporting this notion come from developmental psychology and show that motor performance in childhood can predict executive function in later years of development. For example, Marieke Westendorp and colleagues [17] (University of Groningen, Netherlands) compared 7- to 12-year-old children with learning disabilities to age-matched controls. Both groups of children performed reading, math, motor skill, and object-control tasks. It is not very surprising that the children with learning disabilities performed worse in all tasks than the controls. However, and more important, a positive relationship was observed between reading and locomotor skills and between mathematics and object-control skills, indicating that cognitive skills are not independent of motor performance.

Consider another study testing the causal relation of the previous study. Jan P. Piek and colleagues [18] (Curtin University of Technology, Perth, Australia) demonstrated that early gross motor problems predict later development of executive functions and their dysfunctional development, such as deficits in processing speed and working memory in school-aged children. To summarize, specific learning skills develop later or less well if specific motor skill scores are low in the years before the dysfunctional cognitive performance is recognized. The question of why motor development predicts the development of executive cognitive ability and academic skills is answered from an embodied choice perspective simply by assuming that the body plays its role in cognitive performance.

Within the past decade, the number of studies showing what kind of exercise has an effect on a particular cognitive process has dramatically increased, and applications designed to address acute or chronic deficits in different age groups [19]. For example, Terry McMorris in this work on the history of research into acute exercise-cognition interactions nicely describes in tables all the studies conducted [19]. An illustration of what a typical study looks like may help here to see how this has been studied. David Moreau from Princeton University and colleagues, for example, asked three groups to participate in 8 weeks of aerobic exercise, cognitive training, or a complex sports program that involved both exercise and cognitive components. Improvements from pretest to posttest performances were measured with multiple cognitive tasks involving working memory and mental rotation. Participants in the complex sports program showed the highest improvements in all cognitive tasks, and this has been taken to indicate that training in both aerobic exercise and cognitive skills in a complex sport environment produces what we call embodied choices [20].

However, given that the effect of exercise on cognitive function is not necessarily an indication of embodied choices but might be the result of greater attention capacity or some other explanation, I focus next on movements that *do* change how people solve problem-solving tasks. Karsten Werner, a PhD student of mine, and I once came across a problem-solving task called Maier's two-string problem [21]. Maier hung two strings from the ceiling that a participant was instructed to hold together, but their distance from each other was larger than the participant's arm span. In the room at the time were the following tools that could be used to solve the problem: a chair, a round wooden desk, on the desk a book, a wrench, a wooden plate, and a small dumbbell. Most people in the classic set-up did not easily solve the problem and found some of the tool so useless they did not even try to use them. However, when Maier himself walked by the experimental set-up and "accidentally" touched one of the strings such that it swung forward and backward, participants found a solution: They attached the wrench to one of the strings and swung it such that when they were holding the other string they would be able to catch hold of the string with the wrench on the end of it.

Werner and I designed an experiment in which participants were given different movements beforehand and then asked to attempt the Maier two-string task. Our task had two solutions: As in the original version, the task could be solved by attaching a tool to one string and swinging it; the other solution was to remove all tools from the table, stand on it, and with the higher position be able to grab both strings. Before participants encountered the problem, they were told that we wanted them to warm up before they were tested. One group was asked to perform stepping movements by climbing stairs and another group was asked to move their arms in circles. A third group served as a control group that solved puzzles instead stepping movements or moving arms. We hypothesized that this could be enough to prime participants for one or the other solution. And this is what we found: Participants who moved their arms in circles before they were told to solve the problem used the wrench and a swinging string more often than both those who performed stair-climbing movements and controls, and those who performed stair-climbing movements solved the problem by stepping on the table to reach both strings more often than both those who moved

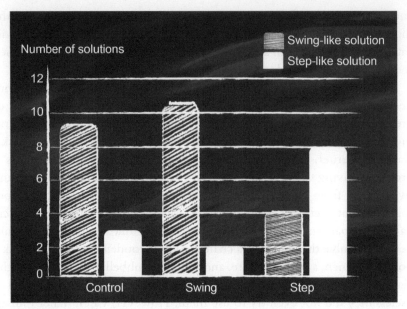

Fig. 4 Number of swing-like and stepping solutions by group.

their arms and controls (Fig. 4) [22]. Later, we showed that the same effect could also be realized when using eye movements to solve problems of that kind [23].

Summing up, higher cognitive processes such as representations of time, finding creative solutions to solving problems, and the choices that are made in these tasks can be framed as embodied choices, and using one's own body seems to be a beneficial strategy for finding solutions. In problem-solving, asking people to relax, take a walk, or sit by a fireplace, under a tree, or in their bathtub can, after some incubation period, produce an "aha" or "eureka" (Greek for "I found it") moment. Thanks to such effects we now know more about benzene rings in chemistry (Kekulé), the law of gravity (Newton), and the principles of water displacement (Archimedes).

Embodied choices when multitasking

Most of our behavior is not purely sequential, allowing us to focus on more than one task. In modern society, the term "second screening" has been coined to describe the practice of watching TV while simultaneously using a smartphone or tablet. This may not be a dangerous activity on your living room couch, but in other situations there are high costs associated with this kind of multitasking, which is why texting while driving, where the potential for causing accidents is well documented, is forbidden [24]. The role of embodied choices in driving has been extensively studied (e.g., by William Consiglio of Miami University and colleagues [25]) with driving simulators, in which braking-response delays or out-of-lane deviations while phoning, typing, or talking can be easily and safely measured. In our own driving simulator study, a post doc Laura Bröker and colleagues asked participants to drive while reacting to important information and ignoring unimportant information presented via headphones. They also manipulated the driving conditions to replicate driving in daylight or with low and high beams at night. As you would expect, driving without having to make a motor response to a distractor was much better, as measured by deviations from the midline of the side of the road they are driving, than when a second task had to be motorically responded to. In the driving simulator, traveling at 100 km/h (about 62 mph) and being asked to brake based on additional information was quite demanding when not much is to see ahead as manipulated by the lighting conditions.

In all conditions, participants who needed to prepare responses to a secondary task were strongly affected by so-called motor interference. It seems that for embodied choices, having to handle two motor tasks at the same task makes it hard to overcome a motor "bottleneck" that tries to sequentially handle motor commands. Even though every driver is aware that the main task is the driving, it seems that doing thing motorically at the same time is different from just distributing your attention to two tasks. I have noticed this when using a GPS navigation system in my car. Checking the navigation screen to see whether I am still on track is different from having to make a route choice—say, when a traffic jam is ahead—by pressing a finger to a small icon on the screen. I have never been in an accident doing this, but following our own research and reading about many other experiments, I simply slow down or ignore the information when traffic is dense or weather conditions do not allow long and stable predictions of the environment.

Another problem most of us face is overconfidence. We think everything always works out, and thus we drive long after our diminished attention capacity or tiredness indicates we should get off the road. When I ask 500 students in a lecture who has a driving license, more or less everybody raises their hand. If I ask who thinks they drive better than the average driver, again most of them raise their hand, even though statistically, they cannot all be better than average! This overconfidence in our own behavior is often beneficial; it helps us to get things done, for example, or plan long-term goals, but for driving, it is dangerous to ignore that multiple tasks that all require motor responses cannot be realized simultaneously in one body.

Discussions about how automated cars will reduce the number of actions required by the drivers seem to suggest that we will solve such problems in the future, but unfortunately, this is only partly realistic. For example, analyses of recent accidents involving automated cars suggest that drivers may have been busy with nondriving tasks and allowed the car to fully take over. If a warning comes from the car, a response to move from one task to another produces what is called switching costs, and stopping one task to start another does takes time. In one of the deadly accidents with a Tesla autopilot driving system, Tesla described the incident as follows: "Huang [the driver] should have had about five seconds, and 150 meters of unobstructed view of the concrete barrier, before the crash. Huang's hands were not detected on the wheel for six seconds prior to the impact. Earlier in the drive, he had been given multiple visual warnings and one audible warning to put his hands back on the wheel" [26]. Given this account and from the literature on embodied choice and motor control on how much time it takes to switch tasks and get vison and hand movements into synchrony in time to react to complex visual stimuli, the accident was a foregone conclusion.

In Germany, the traffic laws were recently changed to allow for fully or semiautomated driving in the future, but I am afraid we need much more knowledge about human behavior and its interaction with such technology before such cars are allowed on the road. On German highways, where many have a speed limit of 130 km/h (about 81 mph) or no limit at all, truck drivers now have distance controls, cruise control, and lane-change alarm if they move too far to the left or right. But these systems require the driver to be ready to take over within a half to 1 second after a warning signal has sounded. If drivers are motorically not prepared for fast choices, as in the Tesla case where the driver did not have hands on the wheel, it seems likely that accident will occur. One colleague studying the habits of truck drivers told me that many power-off these systems because if they do not need to manually attend to the control of the vehicle (steering, speed, etc.) they become much more tired and their attention wanders.

Often we do not even realize how much multitasking influences our attention and performance. My wife, Marei, is quite good at detecting that I am reading or writing emails when we talk on phone and I have given up doing this when she calls. My uncle, a school principal, even made it his hobby to disrupt his pupils' multitasking. He would plant himself in front of students in the hallways between classes so they almost crashed into him if they were walking while fully focused on their smartphone. I am not sure if he has been successful yet in changing their behavior, but the example serves again to point out that our human information processing system has its limits, and if the motor system is involved in typing something on a smartphone, it is not easy to pull attention away from one's fingers and hands, an effect called in psychology the hand-proximity effect.

When does the body malfunction and how do choices change as a result?

Have you ever heard of FOMO? FOMO stands for the fear of missing out and is a new social phenomenon in which predominantly young people believe they cannot survive without their smartphone nearby. FOMO reflects the social pressure people may feel to always be available online or risk being ostracized by their peer group. However, the smartphone is more than a smart object that keeps track of your schedule or tasks. For some, it is an extension of the mind [27], and not only does social fear increase if a person needs to be offline but also the body reacts as well—some start to shiver or feel the vibration of the smartphone even it is not literally there [28]. Here, it is not so much about embodied choices but rather that the smartphone becomes part of the extended mind. Whether it is right to call a smartphone part of the cognitive system is hotly debated [29], but what is clear is that the body that produces actions in an environment is so closely connected to that environment that some researchers even doubt whether it is useful to conceptually separate them [30].

Consider a different bodily dysfunction, the yips. The yips is a shaky movement of the hand that prevents golfers from properly putting a ball even from a short distance. It is like an involuntary hiccup where the wrist moves when it should be still. Some of the great players had the yips, and they tried to compensate by changing their grip, wearing a different glove, or using a broomstick putter. A broomstick putter is just what it sounds like: a very long putter that looks like a broomstick. It fits in the armpit to move the full arm, reducing the responsibility of the wrist. Unfortunately, the International Golf Association recently forbid the use of broomsticks for putting and thus many golfers have been asking for help. This is a big challenge, as the causes of the yips are mostly unknown. Some argue it is a focal dystonia, a dysfunction of the nervous system that produces brain activations that as a consequence produce co-contractions of the muscles that cannot be controlled. A second, more psychological explanation is that golfers are choking under pressure, that in the moment of the swing they are already predicting failure, and in a self-fulfilling prophecy, they shake. Both of these explanations might explain part of the golfers' problem, but studies in our labs and at the German Center for the Yips (run by one of our previous PhD students, Bernd Gerland, himself a golfer who suffered from the yips and now provides training to overcome it) ruled out both explanations. Bernd Gerland ruled out both explanations as for choking under pressure yips affected players should show yips only under pressure but they showed it as well under relaxed and training-like conditions. The focal dystonia explanation was ruled out as neurological tests showed no effector specific (e.g., right arm) focal dystonia that transfers to other tasks. Two ways to compensate for the yips are to change the hand position, for example, to the two-thumb grip, or to use a belly putter (Fig. 5), which seats the end of a slightly longer shaft in the golfer's midriff. As argued above the broom-stick the long putter players were able to fixate at the shoulder is not allowed in official competitions anymore.

Focal dystonia occurs in many fine-tuned hand movements. Examples include writer's cramp and musician's cramp, among others, and it seems to occur in 1% of the population. The yips, depending on the study, affect between 10% and 40% of golfers—even those who are not professional, making overtraining an unlikely explanation. The second explanation—choking under pressure—would suggest that golfers putting in a non-competitive situation without any pressure would be less affected by the yips, but many of the golfers we have seen in our lab continue to show

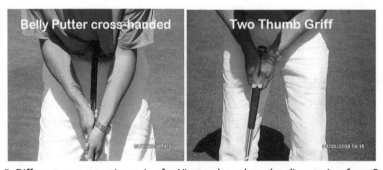

Fig. 5 Different compensation grips for Yippers based on the dissertation from Bernd Gerland (two-thumb griff on the right side of the figure, two-thumb grip).

the wrist movement, and thus choking under pressure may not explain many of the golfers' yips either.

A third explanation we came up with in a team comprising researchers from medicine, music, and sports is based on a motor explanation: We suggested that players condition themselves in a vicious circle [31]. They realize their putting game is getting worse, so they try harder and focus even more on the problem, becoming conditioned to a situation in which they fail and have no way out. They think training harder will solve the problem but it does not in many cases. So how can we help them? For musician's cramp, Botox seems to cure some of the symptoms of the overactive muscles. You may have noticed similar reduced muscle movement in the faces of patients who get Botox injections for cosmetic or other reasons. But although Botox may reduce muscle activation, it has social side effects. For example, participants who had Botox injections had a harder time reading and understanding emotional words or concepts [32]. Given that the yips in golf is most likely a motor problem, motor interventions are more likely to help. For example, Gerland of the German Center for the Yips has golfers who have the yips relearn the putting movement without experiencing the negative effects of failure. He came up with several creative ways to do this. For example, he had clients swing at the ball with a golf club but the ball was actually glued to the ground, or the ball was lifted just before the club made contact with the ball; the club itself might be funny, for example, with a wobbly head that made it near impossible to make a perfect shot; or he might have them perform the golf putt under water. The main point of these exercises is to experience different putting situations in which sinking the ball is not the goal and the wrist movements disappear. Gerland generated these ideas simply by using his own bodily experiences of the disorder. He was certain that the explanations he had been given did not account for his problem and the interventions proposed did not help. All the ideas he generated are embodied choices based on his own yips. The bodily sensations of his own yips let him try to feel and imagine solutions for the cure of yips.

Consider another example, the alien hand syndrome: A hospital patient wakes up and believes that, say, the right arm is not part of their body but alien to them. They insist on that belief even after sensory tests and being asked to move it. The patients instead think the arm would move itself and would like to get it removed.

Another well-known syndrome is phantom pain, which happens to patients who have had an amputation but still feel pain in the amputated limb. Whether such pain occurs seems to depend on whether the pain was there before the amputation. Even after the limb is removed the brain still signals the pain. One researcher at the University of California, San Diego, Vilayanur S. Ramachandran, found that giving patients with phantom pain a mirror in which they could see their existing and healthy arm move as if it was the other, amputated and painful arm allowed them to release the pain from the body [33]. Likewise, the so-called rubber hand illusion is evidence that people can incorporate an artificial rubber hand into their body schema. In this illusion, participants see a rubber hand in front of them covered in such a way that it looks as if it is connected to their body. Their real hand is out of sight of the participants but next to the rubber hand. If both the rubber hand and their own arm are stroked simultaneously, participants feel that the rubber hand belongs to them such that the real hand would move toward the rubber hands' position in space. This sensation is so strong that if the experimenter takes the rubber index finger and bends it radically, the participants feel the pain as if it was their own biological hand [34].

Changes in the perception of the arm happen as well in the so-called giant hand effect in which pilots have reported that their hands seem to grow into giant hands. It has been suggested that the cognitive system is playing a trick to keep pilots from overreacting in case of an emergency and randomly pressing buttons. A similar mind trick is at work when time seems to slow down in near-death experiences, as I can subjectively confirm. Once I was driving to Louisiana State University from New Orleans after a night of no sleep, and I fell asleep. The next thing I knew, I was spinning around in my car on the shoulder next to the highway and grass was hitting my face. Time seemed to pass slowly and without thinking I managed to turn the wheel in a way that allowed the car to stop safely. You can imagine I was wide awake then, but I had no clue how I had used the wheel as a tool to stop the car from spinning, and soon time went back to normal speed. The experience has stopped me from driving without sleep, for sure.

Of course, there are motor dysfunctions that simple interventions cannot cure. Some of these are genetically determined and start in early childhood, such as cerebellar dysfunctions that prevent motor functions from developing normally, as summarized by Leonhard F. Koziol and colleagues:

> *Very preterm birth, defined as less than 32 weeks gestation, is associated with three possible patterns of abnormality in cerebellar development. First, there can be volume reduction of the cerebellar hemispheres and a smaller vermis. Second, there can be volumetric cerebellar hemispheric reduction with an enlarged fourth ventricle and a deformed vermis. Third, there can be normal cerebellar shape but with extensive reduction in its dimensions.*

These types of abnormalities have been associated with a variety of executive functions, cognitive, and motor difficulties. These executive functions, action control deficits are often chronic. Therefore it is clear that perturbations in cerebellum development can often result in "cognitive" deficits. These deficits, and their persistence, may result from the fact that preterm delivery disrupts the developmental program of the cerebellum [35].

Some terminal illnesses, such as Parkinson's disease and multiple sclerosis, among others, damage the nervous system but can appear at first sight to be purely motor disorders, as they influence choices, as proposed by our embodied choice description [36]. Likewise, cognitive dysfunctions such as Alzheimer's disease and dementia, among others, are not purely cognitive dysfunctions, as the motor system suffers as well, and motor training seems to be accepted as one way to counteract the symptoms, as my university and many other research groups have found [37]. Research on social dysfunctions such as autism has also recently returned to embodied explanations, finding that the motor system in people with autism needs to be strengthened to produce social interactions [38]. For example, it has been demonstrated that children with autism reveal abnormal patterns of sensorimotor learning as well as impairment in the execution of "skilled" motor gestures. These deficits correlate with impairment in social and communicative functions. According to Stewart H. Mostofsky and Joshua B. Ewen (Johns Hopkins University School of Medicine, United States), this suggests that in people with autism, deficits in motor production mainly in the cerebellum may contribute to impaired development of social, communicative, and motor capacities [39].

One final example refers to brain damage from accidents or war injuries. A famous example used by the French Philosopher Maurice Merleau-Ponty in 1945 describes the case of a Mr. Schneider. Schneider was a solider in the German Army in World War I and suffered very serious brain injuries after an explosion of a mine. We know about this case as his neurologist provided a detailed report of his behavior. His impairments included a long list of many functions we take for granted, such as loss of visual imagery, loss of body schema, and agnosia, the inability to use sensory input to recognize objects or people. One specific behavior was related to a motor test in which Schneider could grab his nose but not point to it. Merleau-Ponty [40] used this differentiation to argue that intentionality comes in two forms, motor and cognitive:

> It must therefore be concluded that "grasping" or "touching" even for the body, is different from "pointing". From the onset the grasping movement is magically at its completion: it can begin only by anticipating its end, since to disallow taking hold is sufficient to inhibit the action. And it has to be admitted that a point on my body can be present to me as one to be taken hold of without being given in this anticipated grasp as a point to be indicated. But how is this possible? If I know where my nose is when it is a question of holding it, how can I not know where it is when it is a matter of pointing to it? It is probably because knowledge of where something is can be understood in a number of ways.

The Schneider case and many more led to the recognition that indeed we have two separate cortical pathways [41]. Consider, for example, the patient MF that Millner and Goodale from the University of Western Ontario in Canada analyzed. MF was poisoned by carbon monoxide and her ventral pathway was damaged. The ventral pathway is often described as the vision-for-perception pathway for recognizing objects. MFs damage produced a visual form of agnosia, such that she was unable to see the forms of objects properly or to determine whether two visual objects were the same. Most astonishing, her visuomotor functions worked well. If MF was asked to lift an object, her grasping was accurate. She was asked to grab a card and orient it such that it would fit into a slot, like a letter in a mailbox. She was easily able to do that, even though when asked how the slot was oriented, she was unable to say. Another patient, AT, was exactly the reverse. Her dorsal pathway that is often called the perception-for-action pathway was damaged. AT had what is called an optic ataxia; thus in contrast to MF, she was able to see the shape and form of objects but grasping the objects was systematically incorrect. Having a patient who is good at A but not B and another who is good at B but not A reveals what is called double dissociation, that is, that these systems are independent. In another study, apraxia patients who had a motor deficit and were often unable to plan or execute a movement appropriately showed more salient deficits in the pantomime of tool use than during actual use [42].

Further, Bruce Bridgeman, a vision researcher from the University of California in Santa Cruz, showed the same dissociation effects in healthy subjects [43]. Today, researchers tend to argue that dorsal and ventral pathways are not as independent as thought in the 1980s, but damage to different pathways does support the notion that this malfunction prevents the proper functioning of embodied choices. There is ample evidence that choices in finance [44] and health [45] need to be understood from the perspective of embodied choices [46], and that such an understanding can be used to teach risk literacy.

Embodied choices in making financial and health decisions

Embodied choices in health

Earlier I discussed how using simple decision trees in medical decision-making is beneficial relative to a more complex use of cues. Often even a simple calculation of conditional probabilities and remembering what they learned about the risk are problematic for medical doctors, and giving patients only a few minutes to decide between alternative treatments is known to be ineffective, even if it is often the reality in most heathcare systems in the world. How can we ensure better decisions from an embodied choice perspective using the simple heuristics introduced earlier? A well-known example of applying simple heuristics in the medical domain is providing doctors and patients with fact boxes that allow them to make informed decisions, such as those produced by the Harding Center for Risk Literacy in Berlin, Germany [47]. Fact boxes present the available evidence about a topic, say, breast cancer, in an easily understandable manner, often through the use of tables or visualizations that make the information readily accessible to patients and medical personnel alike. A useful guide to making these fact boxes has been published by the Harding Center (Fig. 6) [49].

Most fact boxes help people to get the facts right and provide natural frequencies about the risks associated with getting or not getting vaccines, general health checks, dietary supplements, early detection of cancer, and many other issues. The Harding Center also offers a risk literacy test and feedback that may help people to understand how good their knowledge is [47].

Health is naturally a part of daily activities such as sports or dietary choices. Recently, bodily information has been well studied in food choices, and consumer research journals have produced special issues on that topic [50]. Embodied choices involved in the liking of food have been systematically explored. For example, Ryan S. Elder (Brigham Young University, United States) and Aradhna Krishna (University of Michigan, United States) presented participants with text advertisements for foods that encompassed either a single sense or multiple senses before participants were asked to taste the food. The authors found that taste perception was affected by the externally provided information, such that the food tasted better when the information encompassed several senses. The authors surmised that the advertisement influenced the sensory thoughts during consumption of the food [51]. I remember how in school we were trained to follow the food

Combined whooping cough vaccine

○○○ HARDING CENTER FOR
○○○
○○● **RISK LITERACY**

Numbers for adolescents and adults relating to potential exposure to whooping cough bacteria.

	100 people without combined booster vaccine exposed to whooping cough bacteria	100 people with combined booster vaccine exposed to whooping cough bacteria
Benefits*/**		
How many people get whooping cough?	45–79	3–12
How many people suffer from coughing lasting longer than three weeks due to whooping cough?	36–77	2–12
How many people suffer from vomiting after coughing due to whooping cough?	8–51	1–8

	100 people with tetanus and diptheria vaccination (TD)	100 people with tetanus, diptheria and pertussis vaccination (Tdap)
Harms***		
How many people had a high temperature (over 37.5°C)?		5–33
		No difference
How many people experienced headache?		32–44
		No difference
How many people experienced fatigue?		26–41
		No difference

*Receiving a combined booster vaccine against pertussis also prevents tetanus and diphtheria. **Numbers given under benefits are based on model calculations.
***Redness, pain, or swelling as local side effects around the injection site are possible within 48 hours after vaccination for both types of vaccines.

Shorts summary: The combined whooping cough booster vaccine may prevent getting pertussis after contact with whooping cough bacteria. Redness, pain, or swelling around the injection site are possible. Serve reactions to the vaccination are unknown.

Sources: [1] McIntyre et al. Vaccine 2009; 27(7): 1062-6. [2] Forster et al. In: Berner (ed.) DGPI Handbuch Infektionen bei Kindern und Jugendlichen: Thieme 2013. [3] Doerr & Thraenhart. In: Kark & Werner (eds.). Krebs im Alter. Zur Onkologie und Immunologie im höheren Lebensalter: Steinkopff 1968: 143-47. [4] Mader & Weigerber In: Mader (ed.). Allgemeinmedizin und Praxis: Anleitung in Diagnostik, Therapie und Betreuung. Facharztprüfung Allgemeinmedizin: Springer 2013. [5] Quast. Mitt Osterr Ges Tropenm ed u parasitologie 1998;20:157-64. [6] Wirsing von König et al. Lancet Infect Dis 2003;2(12):744-50. [7] Turnbull et al. Vaccine 2001;19(6):628-36. [8] Van der Wielen et al. Vaccine 2000; 18(20):2075-82.

Last update: April 2016   www.harding-center.mpg.de/en/fact-boxes

Fig. 6 A fact box from the Harding Center for Risk Literacy [48]. *(From https://www. hardingcenter.de/en/fact-boxes. Used with permission from Harding Centre for Risk Competence).*

pyramid that was built to provide us with knowledge about healthy eating. Over time, new research has influenced what we are told to eat and how this is visualized. For example, in the United States, the pyramid of my youth is now "MyPlate." For a historical overview look at, for example, the United State Department of Agriculture food guides of the last decades [52]. From an embodied choice perspective, providing knowledge is not sufficient to change eating behavior. And indeed, in recent years games have been developed that do provide gestures—for example, feeding an alien in a game to learn the content of the food pyramid. Results suggest that such games are effective in fourth-graders, and further research hopefully will continue to test their effects [53].

Often food or drug–use choices are discussed in terms of willpower. For example, whether you are able to withstand drugs [54] or resist eating unhealthy food [55] is a matter of self–control. In a study on embodied choices and willpower, Iris W. Huang (University of Singapore) and colleagues asked participants to make a fist. In contrast to a control group, participants with their hand held in a fist were more likely to decline unhealthy food [55]. What is the explanation for such findings? In general, self–control is often thought to be limited. Roy Baumeister from the University of Queensland, Australia, coined the term ego depletion to describe the idea that self-control functions like a muscle; just as our muscles do not work if we run out of "fuel," we have a limited amount of mental energy and if that is depleted, we do not have enough self-control to reject attractive unhealthy food. Consider two studies that asked participants to choose between cake and fruit salad. Baba Shiv (University of Iowa, United States) and Alexander Fedorikhin (Washington State University, United States) asked participants to choose between chocolate cake and fruit salad. Some participants were placed under cognitive load and required to memorize seven-digit numbers while choosing. The participants with access to fewer self-regulatory resources were more likely to choose the chocolate cake than participants who had a full supply of self-regulatory resources [56]. In another study, Sabrina Bruyneel (Catholic University of Leuven, Belgium) and colleagues sent participants on a mock shopping trip. Given that choosing itself produces ego depletion, some participants had to make a series of product choices, whereas others were given a shopping list and needed only to grab the items (Fig. 7). Only in conditions of very attractive candies, the purchased amount of candies increased when forcing participants to make choices [57].

In sum, embodied choices in the health domain are a meaningful way to improve our decisions, from choosing a medical treatment to exerting self-control in food choices. Changing the way medical information is

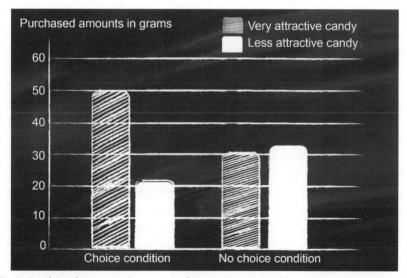

Fig. 7 Purchased amounts (in grams) of very attractive and less attractive candy in the choice condition and in the no-choice condition.

conveyed, advertising food by invoking multiple senses, and embodied games are all ways to generate health-related embodied choices [58].

Embodied choices in finance

It seems that humans are not well equipped and trained to make judgments about, for example, conditional probabilities in finance. Despite major empirical findings on the benefits of intuitive and reflexive processes in making choices, recently the World Bank and the World Institute of Medicine released reports suggesting people should rely on the reflexive system only, without exploring how and when both processes together aid good choices [59]. However and as argued earlier, financial decisions may be affected by perceiving a specific pattern by intuition such as perceiving that the current stock market movements indicates a risk for specific investments. Perception can even vary depending on how important money is to a person. For example, children who are poor perceive coins as larger than children [60] who are rich.

The tendency to go cash-free these days with smartphones, Apple watches, or credit cards may change the way we spend money. I like to play Monopoly with my children, a game in which you buy property and earn money if the other players land on something you own. I like the original version—where the players lay their game money in front of themselves and physically hand over money to pay rent or buy houses and hotels—much more than the new version where each player has a credit card. I do believe that the original version allows for embodied choices: Handling physical money and feeling and seeing how much is left after a purchase may reduce the current tendency toward overspending when money is virtual. It has also been shown in experiments that rapid embodied responses such as approach or avoidance movements can change how much you like a brand or invest in the stock market [61].

In addition, as argued earlier, it has been well established that environmental and personal factors [62] influence context effects (e.g., the same person may have a high tolerance for risk in financial decisions but not for food intake), and that intuitive choices are not good or bad per se but depend on content and context. Furthermore, expertise gained from experience in these choice domains fosters intuitive choices that are embodied, and thus any recommendation relying purely on one decision process or any judgment that promotes only one decision strategy as beneficial is ill-conceived [63].

Consider how you give tips in bars or restaurants. These days when paying with a credit card you are often given the option to calculate a tip yourself or to select a predefined set amount, a flat amount in the local currency or a percentage of the total, maybe 10%, 18%, or 20%. Europeans traveling in the United States might change their usual 10%–20% given there are different cultural norms—we learn by traveling. Recently, however, I read about an interesting study by Rick Van Baaren (Radboud University Nijmegen, Netherlands) and colleagues that has me paying more attention to the servers. They analyzed tipping behavior of guests in restaurants dependent on whether the server mimicked the verbal behavior of the guest (by repeating the guest's order). The results indicate more mimicry earned larger tips [64].

In economics, such social exchanges are often studied in the lab without regard for bodily actions. For example, have you heard about dictator or ultimatum games that are used to test social fairness when you can pay-as-you-wish, as in tips? In those games, participants are invited into the lab and are told that in the next room another participant is involved in the experiment in which the players can leave the experiment with money based on the rules of the game. In the dictator game, one person gets, say, $10 and is asked to say how much they are willing to give to an unknown and unseen participant next door. They can choose between $0 and $10 and whatever they give from the $10 to the participant next door that person can take home, and the remaining can be taken home by the participant making the offer. It's called the dictator game because there is no way to reject the offer given. Recently bodily contact of shaking hands between the experimenter and the participants for longer have been added to this game (in contrast to no hand-shake contact), and thus it serves as another example of embodied choices participants are not aware of.

Subtle smells can influence how much you trust others in one-shot trust games such as a variant of the dictator game I just introduced. In a trust game, Player A decides how much money to send to Player B, and Player B decides how much of the received amount to return to Player A. This game involves trust because Player A has to trust that Player B will send something back. In a one-shot version of the trust game, participants were asked to play a game with another participant who was actually a confederate of the experimenter. The participants each received $5, in 20 quarters. The amount of money the true participant (Player A) sent was quadrupled in value, and the amount the confederate participant (Player B) sent back was also quadrupled. Participants were allowed to pocket what they ended up with. The interesting manipulation was that the participants were instructed to walk to a corner of the room before they ran the game, and the smell in that corner was manipulated. Participants encountered a fishy smell, a fart smell, or no odor. Participants in the role of Player A gave significantly less money in the fishy smell condition than in the other conditions. "Something smells fishy" activated their sense of distrust of Player B [65].

The ultimatum game, however, differs from the dictator game and the one-shot trust game. In this game, Player A has to share a sum of money with Player B. If Player B rejects the offered share, neither player gets anything. But if, for example, Player A offers $3 of a 10-dollar pot to Player B and Player B accepts the offer, both go home with money: $7 for Player A and $3 for Player B. Of course, $3 is more than $0 and any economic model that maximizes value in choices would predict that humans would prefer even $1 to $0. Yet studies have shown that people use fairness as a reason to decline offers that are too low. A person's sex, culture, and altruism have all been shown to influence offers, as well as whether the game is repeated with roles reversed.

The point here is, in contrast to the server-guest interaction, neither bodily information nor any other information about the other person is provided. This is unnatural and quite unlike many social interactions, and it ignores current understanding of the role of the body in social financial exchange from research on small societies [66], families, and peers. Understanding the role of embodied choices in finance has not yet changed the way behavioral experiments are run in economics, but that role is being increasingly acknowledged [67].

Putting yourself in someone else's shoes may help when an investment involves another person's money, say, when investing in stock markets or writing loans and mortgages [68]. For example, Flavia Mengarelli from the Centre de Neuroscience Cognitive, CNRS in France and colleagues showed that feeling responsible for investing the money of others helps people to adjust the risk involved in different investment strategies. I am wondering whether these choices would become better if we would not more and more invest money via computer accounts using recommendations from software not knowing anymore the person and reducing the feeling of responsibility. How embodied choices would help here seems not to have been researched yet.

The 14th-century French philosopher Jean Buridan once asked what a donkey that is equally hungry and thirsty would do when placed precisely midway between a stack of hay and a pail of water. Since the paradox assumes the donkey will always go to whichever is closer, the donkey dies because it cannot make a rational decision between the hay and water. A variant of the paradox substitutes two identical piles of hay for the hay and water, and the donkey dies here as well. I think humans, unlike Buridan's donkey, use their bodily information when confronted with two seemingly identical options of equal distance. As argued earlier, we have dominance in our system, and thus if placed between two options maybe we simply choose the side that is closer to the dominant arm. We could of course mentally roll a die and randomly decide or simply take turns, as our gut feelings simply tell us to feed ourselves.

In sum, financial decisions are not a simple matter of abstract cognitive mathematics where we take even $1 over nothing if an unknown person seems to be unfair. Our bodies influence our choices in real social situations; embodied choice is a behavioral research program so far missing from the menu of economic studies.

References

[1] K. Werner, M. Raab, M.H. Fischer, Moving arms: the effects of sensorimotor information on the problem-solving process. Think. Reason. (2018) https://doi.org/10.1080/13546783.2018.1494630.

[2] A. Frick, M.M. Daum, M. Wilson, F. Wilkening, Effects of action on children's and adults' mental imagery, J. Exp. Child Psychol. 104 (2009) 34–51.

[3] A. Knops, B. Thirion, E.M. Hubbard, V. Michel, S. Dehaene, Recruitment of an area involved in eye movements during mental arithmetic, Science 324 (2009) 1583–1585.

[4] M. Hartmann, L. Grabherr, F.W. Mast, Moving along the mental number line, J. Exp. Psychol. Hum. Percept. Perform. 38 (6) (2012) 1416–1427.

[5] M.H. Fischer, S. Shaki, Number concepts—abstract and embodied. Philos. Trans. R. Soc. B 373 (1752) (2018) https://doi.org/10.1098/rstb. 2017.0125 20170125.

[6] L. Petit, L. Zago, E. Mellet, G. Jobard, F. Crivello, G. Joliot, B. Mazoyer, N. Tzourio-Mazoyer, Strong rightward lateralization of the dorsal attentional network in left-handers with right sighting-eye: an evolutionary advantage, Hum. Brain Mapp. 36 (2015) 1151–1164.

[7] G. Lufityanto, C. Donkin, J. Pearson, Measuring intuition: nonconscious emotional information boosts decision accuracy and confidence. Psychol. Sci.. (2016) https://doi.org/10.1177/0956797616629403.

[8] M.L. Slepian, N. Ambady, Fluid movement and creativity, J. Exp. Psychol. Gen. 141 (2012) 625–629.

[9] M. Oppezzo, D.L. Schwartz, Give your ideas some legs: the positive effect of walking on creative thinking. J. Exp. Psychol. Learn. Mem. Cogn. (2014)https://doi.org/10.1037/a0036577.

[10] American Psychological Association (APA), Taking a Walk May Lead to More Creativity Than Sitting, ScienceDaily, 2014. April 24. Retrieved June 12, 2019 from:www.sciencedaily.com/releases/2014/04/140424101556.htm.

[11] J.H. Kim, Physical activity benefits creativity: squeezing a ball for enhancing creativity. Creat. Res. J. 27 (4) (2015) 328–333, https://doi.org/10.1080/10400419.2015.1087258.

[12] W. Hofmann, R.F. Baumeister, G. Foerster, K.D. Vohs, Everyday temptations: an experience sampling study of desire, conflict, and self-control, J. Pers. Soc. Psychol. 102 (2012) 1318–1335.

[13] See a review fromR. Baumeister, M. Gaillot, C.N. De Wall, M. Oaten, Self-regulation and personality, J. Pers. 74 (2006) 1773–1801.

[14] M. Raab, G. Gigerenzer, Intelligence as smart heuristics, in: R.J. Sternberg, J. Davidson, J. Pretz (Eds.), Cognition and Intelligence, Cambridge University Press, Cambridge, 2005, pp. 188–207.

[15] https://en.wikipedia.org/wiki/Tower_of_Hanoi.

[16] Y.K. Chang, C.L. Tsai, T.M. Hung, E.C. So, F.Z. Chen, J.L. Etnier, Effects of acute exercise on executive function: a study with a Tower of London Task, J. Sport Exerc. Psychol. 33 (6) (2011) 847–865.

[17] M. Westendorp, E. Hartman, S. Houwen, J. Smith, C. Visscher, The relationship between gross motor skills and academic achievement in children with learning disabilities, Res. Dev. Disabil. 32 (6) (2011) 2773–2779.

[18] J.P. Piek, L. Dawson, L.M. Smith, N. Gasson, The role of early fine and gross motor development on later motor and cognitive ability, Hum. Mov. Sci. 27 (5) (2008) 668–681.

[19] T. McMorris, Exercise-Cognition Interaction: Neuroscience Perspectives, Academic Press, Elsevier, London, UK, 2016.

[20] D. Moreau, A.B. Morrison, A.R. Conway, An ecological approach to cognitive enhancement: complex motor training, Acta Psychol. 157 (2015) 44–55.

[21] N.R. Maier, Reasoning in humans: II. The solution of a problem and its appearance in consciousness, J. Comp. Physiol. Psychol. 12 (1931) 181–194.

[22] K. Werner, M. Raab, Moving to solution: effects of movement priming on problem solving, Exp. Psychol. 60 (2013) 403–409.

[23] K. Werner, M. Raab, Moving your eyes to solution: effects of movements on the perception of a problem-solving task. Q. J. Exp. Psychol. 67 (2014) 1571–1578, https://doi.org/10.10180/17470218.889723.

[24] D.L. Strayer, F.A. Drews, Cell-phone-induced driver distraction. Curr. Dir. Psychol. Sci. 16 (3) (2007) 128–131, https://doi.org/10.1111/j.1467-8721.2007.00489.x.

[25] W. Consiglio, P. Driscoll, M. Witte, W.P. Berg, Effect of cellular telephone conversations and other potential interference on reaction time in a braking response. Accid. Anal. Prev. 35 (4) (2003) 495–500, https://doi.org/10.1016/S0001-4575(02)00027-1.

[26] https://www.wired.com/story/tesla-autopilot-self-driving-crash-california/.

[27] A. Newen, L. De Briun, S. Gallagher, 4E cognition: historical boots, key concepts, and central issues, in: A. Newen, L. De Bruin, S. Gallagher (Eds.), The Oxford Handbook of 4E Cognition, Oxford Press, Oxford, UK, 2018, pp. 3–15.

[28] See the book of A. Gazzaley, The Distracted Mind: Ancient Brains in a High-Tech World, MIT Press, Cambridge, MA, 2016.

[29] See Julian Kiverstein (pp. 19–40) inA. Newen, L. De Bruin, S. Gallagher, The Oxford Handbook of 4E Cognition, Oxford Press, Oxford, UK, 2018, pp. 3–15.

[30] A. Chemero, Radical Embodied Cognitive Science, Reprint ed., MIT Press/Bradford Books, Cambridge, MA, 2011.

[31] C. Ioannou, M. Klämpfl, B.H. Lobinger, M. Raab, E. Altenmüller, Psychodiagnostics: classification of the yips phenomenon based on musician's dystonia. Med. Sci. Sports Exerc. (2018)https://doi.org/10.1249/MSS.0000000000001696.

[32] D.A. Havas, A.M. Glenberg, K.A. Gutowski, M.J. Lucarelli, R.J. Davidson, Cosmetic use of botulinum toxin-a affects processing of emotional language. Psychol. Sci. 21 (7) (2010) 895–900, https://doi.org/10.1177/0956797610374742.

[33] See youtube for a demonstration:https://www.youtube.com/watch?v=jNTCFSuKEMA.

[34] M. Botvinik, J. Cohen, Rubber hands "feel" touch that eyes see, Nature 391 (1998) 756.

[35] L.F. Koziol, D.E. Budding, D. Chidekel, From movement to thought: executive function, embodied cognition and the cerebellum. Cerebellum (2001) https://doi.org/10.1007/s12311-011-0321-y.

[36] A. Perugini, J. Ditterich, A.G. Shaikh, B.J. Knowlton, M.A. Basso, Paradoxical decision-making: a framework for understanding cognition in Parkinson's disease. Trends Neurosci. (2018) https://doi.org/10.1016/j.tins.2018.04.006 (Epub ahead of print).

[37] T. Stuckenschneider, C.D. Askew, S. Rüdiger, M. Cristina Polidori, V. Abeln, T. Vogt, … NeuroExercise Study Group, Cardiorespiratory fitness and cognitive function are positively related among participants with mild and subjective cognitive impairment. J. Alzheimers Dis. 62 (4) (2018) 1865–1875, https://doi.org/10.3233/JAD-170996.

[38] SeeA. Hellendoorn, L. Wijnroks, E. van Daalen, C. Dietz, J.K. Buitelaar, P. Leseman, Motor functioning, exploration, visuospatial cognition and language development in preschool children with autism. Res. Dev. Disabil. 39 (2015) 32–42, https://doi.org/10.1016/j.ridd.2014.12.033.

[39] S.H. Mostofsky, J.B. Ewen, Altered connectivity and action model formation in autism is autism. Neuroscientist (2011) https://doi.org/10.1177/1073858410392381.

[40] M. Merleau-Ponty, Phenomenology of Perception, (trans. C. Smith)Routledge and Kegan Paul, London, 2002 Citation from p. 119.

[41] L.G. Ungerleider, M. Mishkin, Two cortical visual systems, in: D.J. Ingle, M.A. Goodale, R.J.W. Mansfeld (Eds.), Analysis of Visual Behavior, The MIT Press, Cambridge, MA, 1982, pp. 549–586.

[42] J. Randerath, G. Goldenberg, W. Spijkers, Y. Li, J. Hermsdoerfer, From pantomime to actual use: how affordances can facilitate actual tool-use. Neuropsychologia 49 (2011) 2410–2416, https://doi.org/10.1016/j.neuropsychologia.2011. 04.017.

[43] B. Bridgeman, S. Lewis, G. Heit, M. Nagle, Relation between cognitive and motor-oriented systems of visual position perception. J. Exp. Psychol. Hum. Percept. Perform. 5 (4) (1979) 692–700, https://doi.org/10.1037/0096-1523.5.4.692.

[44] M. Monti, R. Boero, N. Berg, G. Gigerenzer, L. Martignon, How do common investors behave? Information search and portfolio choice among bank customers and university students. Mind & Society 11 (2012) 203–233, https://doi.org/10.1007/s11299-012-0109-x.

[45] M.A. Jenny, Improving risk literacy, J. Health Manag. 17 (4) (2017) 278–279.

[46] M. Raab, G. Gigerenzer, The power of simplicity: a fast-and-frugal heuristics approach to performance science. Front. Psychol. 6 (2015) 1672, https://doi.org/10.3389/fpsyg.2015.01672.

[47] https://www.harding-center.mpg.de/en.

[48] P. McIntyre, et al., Vaccine 27 (7) (2009) 1062–1066.

[49] M. McDowell, F.G. Rebitschek, G. Gigerenzer, O. Wegwarth, A simple tool for communicating the benefits and harms of health interventions: a guide for creating a fact box, MDM P&P 1 (2016) 1–10.

[50] A. Krishna, N. Schwarz, Sensory marketing, embodiment, and grounded cognition: a review and introduction. J. Consum. Psychol. 24 (2014) 159–168, https://doi.org/10.1016/j.jcps.2013.12.006.

[51] R. Elder, A. Krishna, The visual depiction effect: inducing embodied mental simulation that evokes motor responses, J. Consum. Res. 38 (6) (2012) 988–1003.

[52] https://www.choosemyplate.gov/brief-history-usda-food-guides.

[53] M.C. Johnson-Glenberg, E.B. Hekler, "Alien health game": an embodied exergame to instruct in nutrition and MyPlate, Games Health J. 2 (6) (2013) 354–361.

[54] A. Bechara, Decision making, impulse control and loss of willpower to resist drugs: a neurocognitive perspective. Nat. Neurosci. 8 (2005) 1458–1463, https://doi.org/10.1038/nn1584.

[55] I.W. Hung, A.A. Labroo, From firm muscles to firm willpower: understanding the role of embodied cognition in self-regulation. J. Consum. Res. 37 (2011) 1046–1064, https://doi.org/10.1086/657240.

[56] B. Shiv, A. Fedorikhin, Heart and mind in conflict: the interplay of affect and cognition in consumer decision making, J. Consum. Res. 26 (1999) 278–292.

[57] S. Bruyneel, S. Dewitte, K. Vohs, L. Warlop, Repeated choosing increases susceptibility to affective product features, Int. J. Res. Mark. 23 (2006) 215–225.

[58] O. Petit, F. Basso, D. Merunka, C. Spence, A.D. Cheok, O. Oullier, Pleasure and the control of food intake: an embodied cognition approach to consumer self-regulation, Psychol. Mark. 33 (8) (2016) 608–619. ISSN:0742-6046. https://doi.org/10.1002/mar.20903.

[59] D.E. Melnikoff, J.A. Bargh, The mythical number two. Trends Cogn. Sci. 22 (4) (2018) 280–293, https://doi.org/10.1016/j.tics.2018.02.001.

[60] N.R. van Ulzen, G.R. Semin, R.R. Oudejans, P.J. Beek, Affective stimulus properties influence size perception and the Ebbinghaus illusion. Psychol. Res. 72 (3) (2008) 304–310, https://doi.org/10.1007/s00426-007-0114-6.

[61] See for example:A.I. Alter, D.M. Oppenheimer, Predicting short-term stock: fluctuations by using processing fluency, Proc. Natl. Acad. Sci. 103 (2006) 9369–9372; A.Y. Lee, A.A. Labroo, The effect of conceptual and perceptual fluency on brand evaluation, J. Mark. Res. 41 (2004) 151–165.

[62] R. Frey, A. Pedroni, R. Mata, J. Rieskamp, R. Hertwig, Risk preferences share the psychometric structure of major psychological traits, Sci. Adv. 3 (2017) e1701381.

[63] M. Raab, Motor heuristics and embodied choices: how to choose and act. Curr. Opin. Psychol. 16 (2017) 34–37, https://doi.org/10.1016/j.copsyc.2017.02.029.

[64] R.B. van Baaren, R.W. Holland, K. Kawakami, van, K. A., Mimicry and prosocial behavior. Psychol. Sci. 15 (2004) 71–74, https://doi.org/10.1111/j.0963-7214.2004.01501012.x.

[65] S.W.S. Lee, N. Schwarz, Bidirectionality, mediation, and moderation of metaphorical effects: the embodiment of social suspicion and fishy smells, J. Pers. Soc. Psychol. 103 (5) (2012) 737–749.

[66] J. Henrich, R. Boyd, S. Bowles, C. Camerer, E. Fehr, H. Gintis, Foundations of Human Sociality: Economic Experiments and Ethnographic Evidence From Fifteen Small-Scale Societies, Oxford University Press, Oxford, UK, 2004.

[67] O. Oullier, F. Basso, Embodied economics: how bodily information shapes the social coordination dynamics of decision-making. Philos. Trans. R. Soc. Lond. Ser. B Biol. Sci. 365 (1538) (2010) 291–301, https://doi.org/10.1098/rstb.2009.0168.

[68] F. Mengarelli, L. Moretti, V. Faralla, P. Vindras, A. Sirigu, Economic decisions for others: an exception to loss aversion law. PLoS One 9 (1) (2014) e85042, https://doi.org/10.1371/journal.pone.0085042.

CHAPTER NINE

How do you choose when it is your first time?

I remember when I was 18 years old, which in Germany means you can drive, vote, drink some forms of alcohol, and go to the red-light area in my hometown of Hamburg, well known for its St. Pauli district. I remember some—not all—of these first-time events quite well. For example, I remember being proud to participate in the election of the *Kanzler* (chancellor), the politician who runs Germany. At that time, Helmut Kohl held the office and nationally, most people thought he was doing a good job and should be reelected. But I was raised in Hamburg, a city of 2 million inhabitants that for decades was a hub for Social Democrats, where most people would vote against Kohl. Most of my peer group, being concerned about the climate (yes, already in 1986) and ending reliance on nuclear energy (which actually will happen in Germany in 2022, when the last nuclear power plant will be shut down), were in favor of the Green Party, which was not expected to win the election but could serve as a coalition partner for either the Conservative Party or the Social Democrats. As this was also the end of high school, a time when we were all thinking and talking about the future, I was overwhelmed by the number of arguments for each of the parties (actually there may have been 20 parties in all but only four of them really had a large number of members in Parliament at that time). I remember how I stood in the voting booth knowing that others wanted me to get on with it so they could have their turn, but my stomach was turning somersaults because it was my first vote, and even though I knew my vote would most likely not decide the election, it might have later consequences for what kind of political campaigns I would support. Maybe this led me to focus on just one thought, driven by a gut feeling trying to help me out. I voted for the Social Democrats, knowing that my father was a member, and suddenly I felt that I quite liked a lot of his political statements in our recent discussions and my mind and gut were at ease again. A problem with gut feelings when making first-time choices is that you cannot rely on long experience with that specific choice. So, a transfer from either general principles or a similar situation you have experienced could help. I think in highly personal moments, the gut feeling activates some hidden knowledge stored in your body that drives such choices. By the way, it took 12 more years before the Social Democrats actually won an election.

I believe that these first-time decisions can be easily transferred to any decision in our lives given any decision was once a first-time decision. However, as we age and gain experience, the knowledge of how to choose in different situations allows us to rely more on our gut feelings, and if we are able to listen to our bodies, those choices will be become embodied choices. Of course, a simple way to boost our intuition would be to experience many choices within the same situation. For voting, there is a choice, at least in democracies where elections are held regularly; but would you choose to experience multiple marriages for the sake of making better choices in mating? Maybe that's what Glynn (Scotty) Wolfe, a Baptist minister from California, was up to. At the time of his death in 1997, he had been married 29 times [1]. I doubt that he was any better off with his partner choices for all his experience. The story is different, however, when you make thousands of moves, and the body simply knows when to shoot to the basket versus passing to a teammate.

Climate choices

Costa Rica is one of the countries making a lot of good decisions to protect the flora and fauna, moving faster than most other countries to adopt carbon neutrality. Yet, it is also a popular tourist destination, well known for its primeval forests and wonderful beaches—and filled with guests disturbing the wildlife and leaving garbage, especially plastic. When my daughter spent a year in Costa Rica as an exchange student, the rest of my family and I picked her up and spend 6 weeks in this wonderful country. We realized many of the protective actions came late but were much needed, as you could see how much plastic was still around. I think it had really driven home along with me when I started not only to see the pollution but also to *feel* it while swimming—that's when my body knew it was time to change. Often people have these personal experiences before they become active climate supporters. For example, I am currently sitting in St. Kilda, Australia, a surfing spot near Melbourne, and I can see the campaigns of two surfers walking on the beaches full of plastic and asking for support to remove the mess that many have left. I could imagine how they stepped on plastic, paddled in waves thick with plastic, and that this experience chan-ged their minds and behavior. Larger efforts are now underway to clean the oceans of plastic, such as the work of 4ocean [2]. Maybe to counteract climate change nonbelievers need to have bodily experiences that change their mind and lead to embodied choices, something numbers and pictures seems unable to do.

Sure, preserving the earth is important for our survival and that of future generations, but breathing good air and living in a green environment actually helps the brain. It is quite tragic that despite the huge number of studies indicating the positive effects of being in nature—including boosts to working memory, positive effects on mood, and an increased ability to focus our attention and fight against major illness [3], that humans are not changing easily behavior. For example, an 8-week intervention for urban dwellers that asked a group of participants to spend 10 min a day with nature at least 3 days a week showed reduced stress subjectively as well as measured by reduced cortisol (the stress hormone) compared with a control group [4]. One can see these results not just in one study but in hundreds of them. In a metaanalysis it was found that on average, city dwellers have a 20% increased risk of anxiety disorders and a 40% increased risk of mood disorders compared with people living in less urban areas. At my alma mater, University of Heidelberg in Germany, Andreas Meyer-Lindenberg showed that this is also the case for schizophrenia; he found that the brain changes as a result of living in an urban environment [5]. The consequences of these findings need to be addressed on many levels. Cities and local communities need to fight for more green areas and provide ways for city dwellers to experience nature. The body certainly will react positively, and the reported findings suggest that residents of cities that pursue such changes will have the chance to improve core cognitive and affective functioning.

Moral embodied choices

Metaphors are often used in the context of moral choices, such as "washing one's hands of responsibility." And indeed, studies have shown that the physical act of washing the hands seems to reduce or even remove the feelings associated with moral transgression. The simplest study of this kind was done by researchers Chen-Bo Zhong (University of Toronto, Canada) and Katie Liljenquist (Kellogg Graduate School of Management, Northwestern University, United States), who simply asked two groups of participants to write down past moral transgressions. One group washed their hands and the other group did not. They then filled out a questionnaire about their emotional state and participated in a previously unannounced

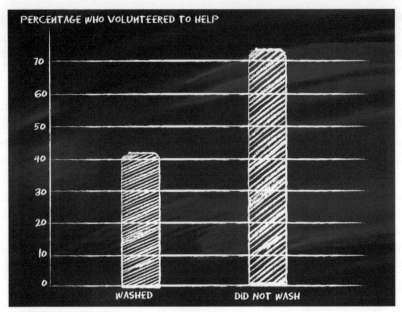

Fig. 1 Percentage of participants who volunteered to help depending on whether they washed their hands.

study (at least this is how the participants are instructed) in which they were tested about their engagement in good deeds. Those who did not wash their hands had a higher propensity to engage in good deeds (Fig. 1) [6].

The effect works, by the way, the other way around as well. Kenworthey Bilz (University of Illinois College of Law, United States) presented "dirty evidence" to law students in a mock trial. Those who heard the dirty evidence were more likely to choose a bottle of hand sanitizer over a pen as a free gift [7]. Studies such as these are not consistent, however, as others found the effect of cleansing reduced the severity of moral judgments or increased moral harshness, or that there was no relationship at all [8].

References

[1] https://en.wikipedia.org/wiki/Glynn_Wolfe.
[2] https://4ocean.com.
[3] G.N. Bratman, J.P. Hamilton, G.C. Daily, The impacts of nature experience on human cognitive function and mental health. Ann. NY Acad. Sci. 1249 (2012) 118–136, https://doi.org/10.1111/j.1749-6632.2011.06400.x.
[4] M.R. Hunter, B.W. Gillespie, S. Chen, S. Yu-Pu, Urban nature experiences reduce stress in the context of daily life based on salivary biomarkers, Front. Psychol. 10 (2019) 722. URLhttps://www.frontiersin.org/article/10.3389/fpsyg.2019.00722.

[5] See the study from Meyer–Lindeberg and many more in this overview:F. Lederbogen, P. Kirsch, L. Haddad, F. Streit, H. Tost, P. Schuch, S. Wüst, J.C. Pruessner, M. Rietschel, M. Deuschle, A. Meyer-Lindenberg, City living and urban upbringing affect neural social stress processing in humans. Nature 474 (7352) (2011) 498–501, https://doi.org/10.1038/nature10190.

[6] C.B. Zhong, K. Liljenquist, Washing away your sins. Threatened morality and physical cleansing, Science 313 (2006) 1451–1452.

[7] K. Bilz, Dirty hands or deterrence? An experimental examination of the exclusionary rule, J. Empir. Leg. Stud. 9 (2012) 149–171.

[8] S. Schnall, J. Benton, S. Harvey, With a clean conscience cleanless reduce the severity of moral judgments, Psychol. Sci. 39 (2008) 1219–1222; D.J. John Son, F. Cheung, M.B. Donnellan, Does cleanliness influence moral judgments? A direct replication of Schnall, Denton & Harvey (2008), Soc. Psychol. 45 (2014) 209–215; C.B. Zhong, B. Strejcek, N. Sivanathan, A clean self can render harsh moral judgment, J. Exp. Soc. Psychol. 46 (5) (2010) 859–862.

CHAPTER TEN

Where do embodied choices come from?

In this chapter, I argue from an evolutionary perspective [1] that cognition, which includes making choices, should be defined as a "situated activity" [2]. Defining choices as a situated activity from what I call a holistic approach is in contrast how traditional basic science approaches describe behavior by looking isolated on one process to explain a very specific subcomponent of behavior. Let me paint the consequences of the traditional basic science approach and propose an alternative holistic approach that describes situated activity.

The Swiss artist Ursus Wehrli cleverly "cleans up" art, by which he means deconstructing an image into its parts and reordering those parts according to shape, color, or some other attribute. For example, Niki de Saint Phalle's volleyball player is deconstructed into a stack of limbs, a stack of circles, a stack of red bits, and so on. Whereas we enjoy this humor in art, in psychology often this is serious business. In the diagnosis or treatment of patients, performing separate measures often gets in the way of making good decisions, as suggested in the simple heuristics discussion. A holistic approach, in contrast to a piecemeal strategy, tries to describe behavior in a more comprehensive way in simple terms, such as in embodied choices.

Let me first separate motor system ontogeny and phylogeny with respect to perception and decision-making, broadly defined. For example, in learning to write, how does the motor system develop with high-level cognitive phenomena (some call this motor cognition ontogeny), and in creativity, how does the motor system evolve together with cognitive function? More specifically, are the cognitive models developed in cognitive science applicable to real environments? Do they help researchers describe and understand realistic decisions when motor behavior is required? As a consequence of knowing the mechanisms of decision-making, can training schedules be altered to optimize performance? Embodied choices reveal the evolutionary links between the motor system, perception, and decision-making. I believe that an embodied choice approach to decision-making will offer a fresh perspective on complex individual behavior and social

Judgment, Decision-Making, and Embodied Choices
https://doi.org/10.1016/B978-0-12-823523-2.00010-6

interaction. The main point I make here is that behavioral flexibility and thus our ability to adapt to changing environments is a property of both bodies and brains. Lambros Malafouris from the Oxford University, United Kingdom, recently argued that human cognition "is made of action and for action" [3], and I could not agree more.

Another hero of mine, the Nobel laureate Niko Tinbergen, summarized four important questions for the study of behavior. What are the proximal mechanisms? How does behavior develop over the course of an individual life? What is the function of behavior that allowed our ancestors to survive? What is the evolutionary history of a specific behavior?

Cognitive psychology has acknowledged all four questions, but, in motor control, the last two questions have been too often neglected. Importantly the two fields have not established working links that could shed light on these questions. For cognitive psychology, there is crucial information about the motor system that is being ignored: Actions are the interface between the self and the environment; they shape our decision-making and facilitate cognitive activity. Therefore I think that exploring the much older (evolutionarily speaking) motor system together with the much younger cognitive system is a valid and necessary approach. In particular, adopting an evolutionary approach that combines both motor ontogeny and motor phylogeny can better explain the complex decision-making.

Let us consider the simplest embodied choice maker: the bacterium *Escherichia coli*, or *E. coli*. *E. coli* has a very simple sensorimotor system with two components to transduce signals from the environment, one slow and one fast. The fast one runs on the order of milliseconds and uses direct perception of its surface receptors to approach attractants and avoid repellents by moving to or away from the perceived environment using rotation or advance movements. The second one runs on the order of seconds and is the *E. coli* memory, as it can use methylation of the occupied receptors to influence its movement direction, as it may be that the bacterium is turning away from a good direction in its current track and needs to remember that food was recently available elsewhere. The interaction and time–sensitive feedback between the slow and fast components allows *E. coli* to make direction decisions without a cognitive map of its spatial environment. The cue from the environment it uses is the chemical concentration of things it likes or dislikes for its survival. The researcher Marc van Duijn (University of Groningen, Netherlands) and colleagues used this example to illustrate that the body of *E. coli* and its simple nervous system provide what seems from the outside to be relatively intelligent behavior [4]. Grounding choices, or in a larger context, cognition in such sensorimotor coordination makes choices embodied as by definition. It seems unlikely that *E. coli* has the same sensations as we have about liking and disliking, and we humans can use multiple senses to orient in our environment and are even able to verbalize where we have been and remember for a long time in episodic memory how it felt. The general principles of simple and embodied choices remain in us, as discussed in the chapter on gut feelings. Even evolutionary researchers have debated whether a larger brain is needed to produce more intelligent behavior, and research has indicated that it is not only brain size (and specifically the recently evolved prefrontal cortex) but the body shape that makes behavior well adapted to the body and its environment.

I have been interested in crows and ravens (*Rabe* in German) ever since I was quite young and my grandfather showed me the Raab family tree and told me the likely derivation of our name. Ravens are similar but not identical to crows. Simply, a crow's tail is shaped like a fan, while the raven's tail appears wedge shaped; ravens travel in pairs, crows in groups. It is no surprise I later loved the novel *Krabat* [5], in which a young boy is magically transformed into a raven. Even while working on my master's in psychology, I was a research assistant to the biological psychologist in our department because of his research interest in crows and their tool use.

New Caledonian crows are large-brained birds and are known for their impressive tool-using abilities compared with others of the crow family, but they show rather comparable performance in tasks not involving tool use. In the 1990s brain size was one explanation of the difference between the New Caledonian crows and others from the same family. However, only in the last 20 years or so it has become obvious that the difference in their bodies makes them better in using tools. Binocular vision and straighter beaks allow them to use tools such as a stick to obtain food that would be otherwise unreachable. The body simply allows for embodied choices compared to other species of the same family who are unable to choose. This does not reject the importance of the brain, even if it seems that brain size itself does not explain the development of cognitive abilities. The fact that brain size differs between men and women but cognitive abilities do not already tells us that it is not the size alone that matters, but there are analyses across the animal world indicating that brain size is a bad predictor of cognition. However, the absolute number of neurons is correlated with cognitive abilities [6], and thus I tell my students to try to avoid destroying too many neurons when hitting the next party. Nevertheless, evolution can only partly explain how to achieve embodied choices, and thus it is important to understand how embodied choices are learned or how we can train to become better at them.

My recommendation to students is based on what neurobiologists know about how the motor system evolved and how this in turn enables the development of cognitive functions—as well how easy it is to stop the brain from developing correctly. But what is the evidence of how embodied choices evolved when we consider organisms with higher cognitive functions than *E. coli*'s movement decisions? You may remember that when I talked about language and its relation to the motor system that the monkey brain areas devoted to the motor system are thought to be equivalent to our Broca's area, which is related to language, and these areas are in the same place in the brain. This is different for the Wernicke's area that is not responsible for speech production but for language development and specific functions such as comprehension of speech (Fig. 1).

And indeed, one of the larger modifications of the human motor system is the emergence of Broca's area. Some researchers argue the emergence of Broca's area is due to changes in the left ventral premotor cortex that are responsible for speech production [7]. Change in only the left and not in the right ventral premotor cortex is important, as it is additional evidence of having a motor system asymmetry, as discussed before for the development of handedness. For example, great apes seem to be right handed when using tools [8], and right-handed chimpanzees have a greater hemispheric asymmetry compared with ambidextrous chimpanzees. Having an arm that is dominant allowed the development of one hand free for gesturing and later spoken language as we know it, which allows having both hands free for something else [9]. The evidence I reported above on language and the

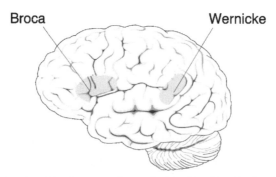

Fig. 1 Language-related brain areas. *(From National Institute on Deafness and Other Communication Disorders, https://www.nidcd.nih.gov/health/aphasia).*

motor system (e.g., that the action word "lick" activates the motor representation of the tongue) has been used as evidence that speech developed from the motor system and acknowledge the importance of the motor system for higher cognitive processes such as language or choices [10]. An important effect was found by Thomas H. Bak (Medical Research Council's Cognition and Brain Sciences Unit, United Kingdom) and colleagues showing that in patients in whom the motor neurons are dysfunctional, action words are more affected than nouns [11].

The afore-mentioned studies suggest that even though the motor system originally evolved to prepare and control movements, it is also active in language and judgments. For example, a study by Ranulfo Romo (National Autonomous University of Mexico) and colleagues showed that in a discrimination task involving two stimuli, the premotor system was involved in signaling the perceptual decision to higher cognitive areas [12]. Why this evolution happened in the way it did is hard to defend with one argument but I personally like the following, which confirms what I have been saying about embodied choices. In childhood, our own motor behavior was often related to how we or others changed something in the environment. In short, complex behavior was always established by our own or others' actions [13]. In other words, our representation of the world comes about by acting in the world, as many researchers, such as Andy Clark [14] from the University of Edingburgh and Lawrence Barsalou [15], from the University of Glasgow have described in their writings.

References

[1] L. Barrett, R. Dunbar, J. Lycett, Evolutionary Psychology, Princeton University Press, Princeton, NJ, 2002.
[2] M.I. Anderson, Embodied cognition: a field guide, Artif. Intell. 149 (2003) 91–130.
[3] Lambros Malafouris (p. 767)A. Newen, L. De Bruin, S. Gallagher (Eds.), The Oxford Handbook of 4E Cognition, Oxford Press, Oxford, UK, 2018, pp. 755–771.
[4] M. Van Duijn, F. Keijzer, D. Franken, Principles of minimal cognition: casting cognition as sensorimotor coordination, Adapt. Behav. 14 (2006) 157–170.
[5] https://en.wikipedia.org/wiki/Krabat_(novel).
[6] S. Herculano-Houzel, Numbers of neurons as biological correlates of cognitive capabilities, Curr. Opin. Behav. Sci. 16 (2017) 1–17.
[7] J. Kaas, Evolution of somatosensory and motor cortex in primates, Anat. Rec. A Discov. Mol. Cell. Evol. Biol. 281 (2004) 1148–1156.
[8] E.V. Lonsdorf, W.D. Hopkins, Wild chimpanzees show population-level handedness for tool use, Proc. Natl. Acad. Sci. USA 102 (2005) 12634–12638.
[9] W.D. Hopkins, J.L. Russell, C. Cantalupo, Neuroanatomical correlates of handedness for tool use in chimpanzees (Pan troglodytes): implication for theories on the evolution of language, Psychol. Sci. 18 (2007) 971–977.

[10] O. Hauk, I. Johnsrude, F. Pulvermüller, Somatotopic representation of action words in human motor and premotor cortex, Neuron 41 (2004) 301–307.

[11] T.H. Baka, J.R. Hodgesa, The effects of motor neurone disease on language: further evidence, Brain Lang. 89 (2004) 354–361.

[12] R. Romo, A. Hernandez, A. Zainos, Neuronal correlates of a perceptual decision in ventral premotor cortex, Neuron 41 (2004) 165–173.

[13] M. Johnson, The Body in the Mind: The Bodily Basis of Meaning, Imagination, and Reason, University of Chicago Press, Chicago, IL, USA, 1987.

[14] A. Clark, Being There: Putting Brain, Body and World Together Again, MIT Press, Cambridge, MA, 1997.

[15] L.W. Barsalou, Grounded cognition, Annu. Rev. Psychol. 59 (2008) 617–645.

CHAPTER ELEVEN

How can embodied choices be trained?

An important avenue for improving embodied choices is to provide embodied learning experiences. For example, Robin Hogarth from Barcelona Graduate School of Economics in Spain argued that to establish intuitive thinking, which we have seen is related to gut feelings, we need to learn implicitly [1]. Implicit learning refers to a learning experience where there is little effort or conscious awareness that we are learning. Consider the learning of language. As a child you learn your native language day-by-day through listening, testing, and producing sounds without full explicit knowledge of all the grammar rules of that language. In contrast, learning a second language in school is much more effortful and conscious, often involving memorizing vocabulary, lists of verb tenses, and unfamiliar grammatical rules and later using that explicit knowledge to produce sentences.

Following Hogarth's concept, we should allow for performance errors and for high-quality feedback to establish good learning. However, there are other forms of intuitive learning that avoid producing too much explicit learning by errors. For example, imagine you want to learn how to play miniature golf, which Rich Masters has suggested is best attempted with an errorless learning procedure. How does that work? You place the ball only 1 inch away from the hole and putt. If you are successful, you increase the distance and repeat, and so on. This strategy reduces hypothesis testing for the motor system, such as deciding whether to change your grip or the force of your swing if the putt was too short. If you later find yourself under stress, say, in the World Cup final or just trying to win a game with friends, you are at less risk of overloading your working memory system when performing those movements than those who test a lot of hypotheses during the learning phase [2]. Indeed, in the study by Masters, people performed better when they relied on errorless learning that promotes implicit learning. Given, as noted earlier, that implicit learning is the foundation of intuitive processes, the embodied choices of the motor system informing how to putt produced those findings. Anecdotally, it has been reported that if tennis players who are beginning to lose congratulate their opponent when switching sides and ask how they made that wonderful return, the opponent will begin to lose. Explicitly thinking about movements that had been working fine without any deliberation may cause the opponent to start making poorer returns. Too much attention to one's movements is not always beneficial [3].

We discussed earlier how metaphors connect language and movement. Metaphors (and analogies) have also been used in teaching a skilled movement. For example, one of my previous PhD students, Nele Tielemann (published in later publications with the name Schlapkohl) and colleagues, designed an experiment in which participants were assigned to an analogy condition or a movement description condition to learn how to hit the forehand topspin in table tennis. In the analogy condition, participants were told that hitting the ball should be like running their hand up a stair banister. In the movement description condition, participants received a textbook description of the skill. Results indicate that the analogy produced better movements and more successful hits than the textbook instructions. One explanation was that the analogy instruction produced a visual image of the movement that was learned implicitly (revealed by interviewing the learners about their knowledge of the movement after training) and also was more robust against stress, such as time pressure or making a decision about where to place the ball [4].

Embodied choices in educational settings

Remember when you were in school or college? Did you pay attention to every lesson, or did your mind sometimes wander? Not staying on task has been shown in lab experiments to be detrimental to performance, affecting school grades, and retention. But recently, studies found that unintentional mind wandering in class may actually be beneficial to your task performance. For example, Jeffrey Wammes (University of Waterloo, Canada) and colleagues tested undergraduates in a physiological psychology course and found that those students whose mind wandered a lot unintentionally actually unconsciously worked more on the content and had better quiz scores than those who stayed focused or engaged in an intentional mind-wandering task [5]. Whether gut feelings formed during these moments influenced the choice of an answer in a quiz is hard to know, but there are other studies indicating there are benefits to involve the body in learning. For example, in learning math, vocabulary, learning the clock time, and many other subjects and skills, children seem to benefit from not sitting in their chairs but actually moving around in ways that foster the learning of the specific content [6].

In our own lab, we tested primary school children who were ready to learn how to tell the time of a clock. One group of children learned in the traditional way by being given handouts depicting various clocks showing specific times and answering questions, such as, "Leo wakes up at 7; which of the clocks show 7 o'clock in the morning?" Another group received the same content but in an app that allowed them to move the clock hands. A third group used even more of their body. They received the same content but were asked to stand up and imitate the correct position of the clock hands, using both arms. Tests before and after learning revealed that imitating the clock with the body produced the best performance, indicating that when asked to perform a cognitive task such as memorizing representations of time, embodied choices are of value (Fig. 1).

Learning embodied choices

How do we learn embodied choices? Here, an example from daily behavior provides two more or less different answers to that question. One way of thinking assumes that the environment provides us with a field of multiple affordances. For example, a hand extended to you affords you an

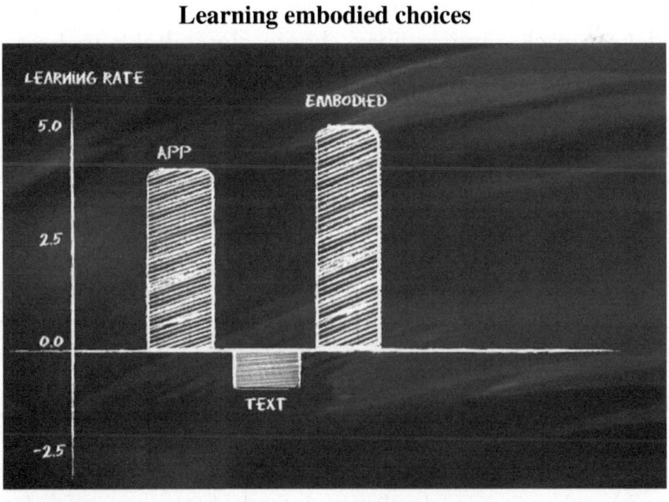

Learning embodied choices

Fig. 1 Learning rate (based on performance of correct solutions in telling time tasks) for clock reading for three different learning conditions [7].

opportunity to shake it in most social situations. Whose hand you choose to shake and when to shake can even "go viral" on the Internet. If you happen to be Prime Minister of France shaking hands with a Yellow Vest person at the airport that wears the yellow vest as part of his working suit but not shaking hands with an opposing Yellow Vest demonstrating against your policies is a choice of milliseconds often directly controlled by routines of your body. If you are the British Prime Minister declining to shake the hand of a policeman outside 10 Downing Street after another world leader has just done so this gets viral in the internet and again was a direct consequence of routine bodily behavior. This affordances way of thinking is often referred to as direct perception. The perception–action link and cognition are closely tied, and it may not even make sense to talk about representations of actions as they happen in the moment of time. An alternative approach assumes shared representations of perception and action, and argues that in the case of an approaching hand, you can predict the movement based on your own movement experiences and using a common code of shared perception-action representation, make the right movement and grab the approaching hand [8].

In a study on boxing, it was found that there is an optimal distance between the heavy bag and the person punching it. This distance allows boxers to train multiple movements, such as jabs and uppercuts, among others [9]. Consider now a much more complex and risky task: ice climbing. In ice climbing, not only do experts use more distant holds and display different kinematics from novices, but also exhibit a difference in using their embodied choices when climbing up and finding a route [10]. Earlier, I described how rock climbers may choose closer holds to be safe, even though they look at more distant holds. Given the findings on embodied choices, one might expect the same for ice climbers, given that at least for novices, this sport is quite challenging. More important for the embodied choice claim is that all climbers not only anticipate the next step or hold but also preplan multiple steps ahead, just as good chess players spend more time planning their moves than actually moving the pieces.

In a study on climbing in our lab, we asked whether these motor experiences of climbing would also enhance planning processes in general. First, we tested children of different ages in whom we knew the planning processes are just developing and correlate with their motor abilities. Thus those who have a good motor ability score well and have high scores in cognitive planning. We then trained the children to climb a fixed route (so only motor control but no planning involved), climb freely (so motor control and planning involved), and plan a route (so no motor control involved). Informed by the science of development, we predicted that in climbing, both motor control and cognitive planning (finding a route) would lead to embodied choices, such that even training only the motor components would facilitate cognitive planning processes and thus allow better choices in unrelated planning tasks [11]. Another manipulation we did was to change the children's perception of their own body as they climbed up a wall. In one condition, they received heavy vests that made them heavier than they actually were, and in another condition we connected their arms and legs to their back with elastic cords, making stretching and reaching a much harder task. As you can imagine, these changes to their body changed not only which holds they decided to grasp but also how they planned to move ahead [12]. In the future, we plan to program the robots with movements and how the children learned. Researchers in the field of developmental robots are now trying to allow robots to change their bodies, for example, growing larger as children do and changing their body schema by learning [13].

Using intuition to predict sports outcomes

Try this experiment: Ask self-described basketball experts before an actual basketball game to predict the outcome. Please ask half of these experts to analyze and list the reasons for their predictions, and instruct the other half not to analyze their reasons but to predict intuitively. Your findings may match the findings of existing studies showing that deliberate reasoning results in fewer correct predictions [14]. Why would this be? One explanation of why thinking too much leads to poorer predictions is that people use too much information that is not valid. For example, an expert might get caught up thinking through how each team has dealt with injuries in the past and make assumptions that have no bearing on the game about to be played.

Henning Plessner (University of Heidelberg, Germany) asked Germans to predict game outcomes of the World Cup in soccer either a couple of weeks before the tournament or 1 week before. Those who bet a couple of weeks before were better off, as more information and less valid information about teams is available just a week before the games [15]. This may partly explain the lucky rookie effect: The lucky rookie is the person who, having never shown much knowledge or even interest in the sport, wins bets on game outcomes. These rookies are often people who use just one piece of information in the recognition heuristic, as described earlier, that is, whether they have heard something about the team or not.

Often less but very valid information can outperform a lot of information. In one of my seminars, students were asked to predict the next weekends' soccer games given the information that is presented in soccer statistics and soccer journals, such as the current rank in the league table, goals, goals against, goal difference, wins, losses, draws, home advantage, the size of the stadium and city, and much more. We found that using less of the data produced better predictions of the actual outcomes [16]. Looking at the specific equations they used to weigh and combine information, the simpler solutions were the most beneficial, and this held whether they worked alone or in small groups.

My colleague Philipp Philippen and I showed that models that predict the ranks and numbers of medals for each country in the Olympic games using multiple sets of data do not perform as well as our simple model that uses the previous rank and number of medals won in the previous Olympics. One of the reasons is that in sports, previous success breeds current success, but another reason is that all the factors used to predict the number of medal wins are quite stable. Colleagues at Harvard University (United States) [17] and Hamburg University [18] (Germany) have been very creative in considering socioeconomic variables such as the gross domestic product of a country or even detailed data for winter game predictions such as the percentage of snow-covered countryside relative to the total size of the country and the days of snow cover of this percentage over a year. But you would be correct to guess that the simple model Philippen and I analyzed outperformed the much more complex predictions by far [19].

Using tools in embodied choices

Tools support our daily actions and one can hardly imagine what life would be like without them. Even in the Stone Age, our prehistoric ancestors had tools. You will also find many examples of clever tool use in animals, from birds to bonobos and many other species that use tools to get food [20]. Neuroscientists have suggested that the brains of animals and humans [21] adapt to the tools being used, and our peripersonal space is enlarged by the size of the tool we are trained on to reach a target [22]. For example, in Japan a research team lead by Tetsuro Matsuzawa at the Primate Research Institute of the Kyoto University trained monkeys for 2 weeks and the monkeys learned to use a rake to pull food closer to them. A study found that in the monkeys' brain, those neurons that were associated with activation for visual stimuli near the hand extended in their brain area related to grasping to the length of the tool as it would be part of their body schema.

Chimpanzees are also very clever and have shown to be better than humans at many tasks. I once made a research visit to the Primate Research Center [23] at Kyoto University in Japan and was able to be part of a team testing the embodied choices of a few chimpanzees. One of them, Ai, is incredibly good at memorizing numbers. After training, she and I both did a test. Nine digits were spread across a touchscreen. After the first number was touched, all the numbers were masked. The task was to remember where the next higher number was and press on it, continuing until all the remaining masked numbers had been located (Fig. 2).

Well my error rate was high and I was slow. If you look at videos of Ai on the Internet or provided by the Primate Research Center, you will see Ai producing these patterns that randomly change from trial to trial with no errors and at a rapid pace—multiple times faster than my performance.

When I tested other chimpanzees of the same troop, a large gray male made sure to let me know that he was the boss in town, jumping against the window that, to my luck, separated us when females were around. I understood and made myself smaller, as my Japanese colleagues were smaller than I, and the chimpanzee had seen in me the biggest threat. In addition, I had a gray beard and thus looked a bit like a silverback attacker. I think it was clear to the chimpanzee that the large ape (me) would be the first to attack to make sure that all was his. One of the Japanese research scholar put on a set of

Fig. 2 Chimpanzee Ai during her test. *(Photo by Tetsuro Matsuzawa, Kyoto University. (https://fpcj.jp/en/assistance-en/tours_notice-en/p=59743/).)*

plastic vampire teeth and made clear to them (or me) that it was she who should be most feared. I also realized that when I was the experimenter, it was more of them testing me; if I made the task more difficult but gave them the same amount of food, they correctly complained. Once I even forgot to give food after a correct trial and immediately the chimpanzee knocked at the window and pointed to the food box and the opening in which I put the food, to remind me to focus on my job.

Although it is clear that animals are clever, they certainly have a different cognitive system. Their embodied choices seem to involve moving their hands in support of memorizing spatial location, just as we sometimes memorize our bank account code better when we type it in mental simulation with our fingers. An evolutionary benefit of memorizing objects in space (even numbers, which for the chimpanzees were not in any way meaningful) became clear from the work a former colleague of mine at the Max Planck Institute for Human Development in Berlin [24]. Andreas Wilke (now at Clarkson University, United States) and colleagues found that animals are quite good at remembering spatial places because they need to come back to those that are rich in food or possible mates, and they even remember places in sequence or clumps of places that would offer more resources. Wilke argued that this may be the origin of why we try to see patterns in the world. Consider the hot hand phenomenon in basketball, in which a player who has made a series of baskets is thought to have a better chance at continued success.

In humans, anecdotal and self-reported evidence suggests that humans perceive an artificial leg to be part of their own body, or that skis become part of the body experience after many years of training. Changing a golf club or a tennis racket can be a nightmare for athletes. A movie about Björn Borg shows the famous tennis player touching and selecting his racket very carefully, listening to his own body on whether it fits well. These stories support the claim that humans and animals embody a tool in such a way that it becomes part of the extended space within the motor cortex.

When using a tool, it seems that we plan ahead how to use it and thus embodied choices predict those behaviors. For example, David Rosenbaum and colleagues showed that people grab objects depending on what to do with them next. This is what Rosenbaum from the University of California, Riverside, called the end-state comfort effect. Remember the wine glass taken from the shelf in Chapter 5? If you were planning to drink from it, rather than just moving it, you would grab it in an uncomfortable way—thumb down—and rotate it midair to achieve end-state comfort at the end of the movement [25]. This seems to develop quite early in childhood and is another way the body affects how we choose to grasp tools or objects [26]. Elisabeth Pacherie from the CNRS, Paris in France coined the phrase motor intentionality [27]. Simply put, it means that we use what we intend to do with objects to activate specific motor representations. Are you planning to pour that wine now or put the glass out for later? Here you can recall the affordances discussed earlier: The wine glass provides you with the affordance to grab it, but the intention drives how you grab it.

I remember the first time I used welding to bond metal. When I was about 14 or 15 years old our high school asked us to do a 4-week internship in industry to experience early-morning hard work in factories or small companies. I chose a car repair shop. Well, I was not much help except in changing oil or tires. The upside of this was that I was allowed into the car junkyard. I had two ideas. First, I used an angle grinder to remove the back of a Volkswagen Beetle from the rest of the car. My plan was to put it on the wall in my room, put drinks in the trunk compartment, and open the trunk and have the rear lights go on when someone wanted a drink. I managed to split the car and move it to my room, but it was too heavy for the wall and thus I kept my bar on the floor.

The second idea was to build an iceboat. I would produce a metal skid, connect my windsurfing board to it, put my sail and a wishbone boom on the mast, and my iceboat would be ready. The main thing was to build the skid with good runners for the ice. I used welding equipment that required me to hold the welding gun in one hand and the material to connect two pieces of metal in the other. The problem was that the protective welding mask was heavy and had to be held with a hand too. So my plan was to ignore the mask and just peek at what I was doing with as little eye contact as possible because I had been told that looking at the process unprotected was dangerous for the eyes. And it was. For 2 days, I was unable to see anything and was helpless to find my way around the house. It was one of the most frightening experiences of my life, but it made me take better care of my body, that is, at least for 2 more years. Remember the ACL (anterior cruciate ligament) injury I had when I was a volleyball player? I failed to mention that the injury was the result of getting a ride from a motorbike tied with a long rope to my skateboard that did not end well. My eyesight after the welding incident recovered and I managed to finish the ice yacht and used frozen lakes to ice sail or surf. You would not be surprised if I told you that I forgot to put brakes on the iceboat, but that is a different story.

Using implicit learning to improve embodied choices

I presented earlier one specific way to learn that may help us trust and use our gut feelings and thus produce embodied choices: implicit learning. I expand on this here. I already argued that intuitive (as opposed to deliberate) decisions are fast decisions that are based on a perceived pattern of information activating a specific action or set of actions. However, routine behavior is not the same as intuitive processes, as we have a choice beyond reflexive behavior. Hogarth argued that the link between intuitive processes when deciding and the preference to use these (as opposed to deliberative) processes is derived from tacit (implicit) information accumulated over long-term experience, such as the details of your native language grammar, which you may not be able to verbalize but can still use appropriately [1].

I apply what my colleagues Judith Orasanu and Teddy Connolly [28] believe to be the seven key components of a decision to the domain of sports. Note that not every decision situation will include all seven of these stages, but they are particularly relevant to the sports domain. The sports domain offers a chance to explore real-world decisions, made by motivated and experienced agents, in rich environments under various conditions (e.g., uncertainty and time pressure). We in sport psychology take advantage of this natural opportunity to study decision-making that occurs outside the lab, on the playing field.

The first step in a decision-making is the presentation of the problem. While this may seem a trivial or obvious "step," it is actually the focus of a great deal of research in judgment and decision-making—such as work on framing effects [29]. That is, the subsequent steps of a decision are not independent of the manner in which a decision is encountered, or the way it is presented. Step 2 is the identification of the constraints, resources, and goals facing the decision maker. These properties can be specific, such as limited time or information available, or they can be abstract, such as the goal of maximizing expected payoff. In Step 3, the generation of possible solutions to the problem, or courses of action, occurs. This step in particular may not be relevant to many laboratory decision-making tasks, where participants are often presented explicitly with the options from which they must choose.

Step 4 of the decision-making protocol, consideration of possible solutions is the one typically regarded as representing the whole of the decision-making process. This implies that the first three steps are often taken for granted—if they are appreciated at all—in much decision-making research. Similarly, the next two steps are rarely dissociated from the output of the consideration phase. Selection of a course of action is generally seen as synonymous with identifying the "winner" of the consideration phase (Step 5); and initiation of the selected action is almost always seen as a straightforward extension of a mentally selected option to a physically realized one (Step 6). Finally, Step 7 of a decision protocol is the evaluation of the decision made, including the appraisal of feedback information, if any exists.

I offer a brief sports example to illustrate each of these seven steps. Imagine a forward in soccer who is dribbling toward the goal and is approached by a defender. At this point, the decision problem has presented itself: what action should the forward take in response to the approaching defender? The forward identifies the behavioral constraints (e.g., passing offside is not an option) and prioritizes the goals (e.g., above all, retain possession, but score if possible). In light of these, the forward generates possible options that can be undertaken, such as shooting at the goal, passing to a wing player, or dribbling away from the defender. The forward considers these courses of action, perhaps by ranking them according to their likelihood of achieving the top goal (retaining possession), and then selects an action; this is likely to be the one with the highest rank. The forward initiates the action by physically performing so as to bring about the selected action (e.g., physically dribbling the ball to the right). This buys time for the wing player to streak toward the goal and be in place to receive a passed ball and assist in a score—resulting in positive evaluation of the forward's decision. Implicit learning can now be applied to all these different steps in one training or separate trainings that, say, focus on perception and manipulate the presentation of the problem to be addressed.

Changing the environment or adapting to it

In the 2017 tragedy that occurred in the Grenfell Tower apartments in London, firefighters were confronted with what they called "their awful choice on the stairs": the "terrible dilemma" of choosing between helping a terrified mother in the 10th-floor stairway or going up to the 14th floor where people were trapped. This human tragedy caused a profound societal impact. As I have presented earlier, temperature and many more environmental factors influence our judgments. Choosing to set the temperature of a room such that it does not bias people's choices in one or the other direction is different from the situation the firefighters faced, as they could

not change much of the environment they found themselves in; thus training them was the most important adaptation to make. I will now provide
some general ideas on how embodied choices can be trained in the next
chapter.

References

[1] Hogarth, R. M. (2001). *Educating Intuition*. Chicago, IL: The University of Chicago
    Press.
[2] Maxwell, J. P., Masters, R. S. W., Kerr, E., & Weedon, E. (2001). The implicit benefit
    of learning without errors. *Q. J. Exp. Psychol.*, *54A*(4), 1049–1068.
[3] Wulf, G. (2013). Attentional focus and motor learning: a review of 15 years. *Int. Rev.
    Sport Exerc. Psychol.*, *6*, 77–104.
[4] Schlapkohl, N., Hohmann, T., & Raab, M. (2012). Effects of instructions on perfor-
    mance outcome and movement patterns for novices and experts in table tennis. *Int. J.
    Sport Psychol.*, *43*(6), 522–541. https://doi.org/10.7352/IJSP2012.43.053.
[5] Wammes, J. D., Seli, P., Cheyne, J. A., Boucher, P. O., & Smilek, D. (2016). Mind
    wandering during lectures II: relation to academic performance. *Scholarsh. Teach. Learn.
    Psychol.*, *2*, 33–48.
[6] Bresler, L. (2004). *Knowing Bodies, Moving Minds: Towards Embodied Teaching and Learn-
    ing*. Boston: Kluwer Academic Publishers.
[7] Loeffler, J., Raab, M., & Cañal-Bruland, R. (2020). Let's do the time warp again—
    embodied learning of the concept of time in an applied school setting. *Interact. Learn.
    Environ.*. https://doi.org/10.1080/10494820.2020.1789669.
[8] Raab, M., & Araujo, D. (2019). Embodied cognition with and without mental repre-
    sentations: the case of embodied choices in sports. *Front. Psychol.*, . https://doi.org/
    10.3389/fpsyg.2019.01825.
[9] Hristovski, R., Davids, K. W., & Araujo, D. (2009). Information for regulating action
    in sport: metastability and emergence of tactical solutions under ecological constraints.
    In D. Araujo, H. Ripoll, & M. Raab (Eds.), *Perspectives on Cognition and Action in Sport*
    (pp. 43–57). Hauppauge, NY: Nova Science Publishers.
[10] Seifert, L., Wattebled, L., Herault, R., Poizat, G., Adé, D., Gal-Petitfaux, N., et al.
    (2014). Neurobiological degeneracy and affordance perception support functional
    intra-individual variability of inter-limb coordination during ice climbing. *PLoS
    One*, *9*(2), e89865. https://doi.org/10.1371/journal.pone.0089865.
[11] See papers showing that climbing requires both complex cognitive planning such as in
    Cascone, S., Lamberti, G., Titomanlio, G., & Piazza, O. (2013). Pharmacokinetics of
    Remifentanil: a three-compartmental modeling approach. *Transl. Med. UniSa*, 7, 18–
    22. Motor planning such as in Testa, M., Martin, L., & Debû, B. (2003). 3D analysis of
    posturo-kinetic coordination associated with a climbing task in children and teenagers.
    Neurosci. Lett., *336*(1), 45–49.
[12] Musculus, L., & Raab, M. (2019). What happens before and when children decide? A
    systematic review on the development of decision-making processes. In B. Strauss, B.
    Halberschmidt, T. Utesch, D. Dreiskämper, S. Brückner, M. Tietjens, V. Storm, L.
    Schücker, F. Rosenfeld, C. Raue, S. Mentzel, M. Kolb, L. Henning, & L. Busch
    (Eds.), *Abstract book: 15th European Congress of Sport & Exercise Psychology, Münster, Ger-
    many, 15-20 July 2019* (p. 50). Münster: Department of Sport and Exercise Psychology,
    University of Muenster.
[13] Bongard, J., Zykov, V., & Lipson, H. (2006). Resilient machines through continuous
    self-modeling. *Science*, *314*, 1118–1121.

[14] Halberstadt, J. B., & Levine, G. M. (1999). Effects of reasons analysis on the accuracy of predicting basketball games. *J. Appl. Soc. Psychol.*, *29*, 517–530.

[15] Plessner, H., & Czenna, S. (2008). The benefits of intuition. In H. Plessner, C. Betsch, & T. Betsch (Eds.), *Intuition in Judgment and Decision Making* (pp. 251–265). New York, NY: Erlbaum.

[16] Gröschner, C., & Raab, M. (2006). Wer wird Deutscher Meister? Deskriptive und normative Aspekte von Vorhersagemodellen im Sport. *Z. Sportpsychol.*, *13*, 23–36.

[17] Johnson, D., & Ali, A. (2004). A tale of two seasons: participation and medal counts at the summer and winter games. *Soc. Sci. Q.*, *84*(4), 974–993.

[18] Meannig, W., & Wellbrock, C. (2008). Sozioökonomische Schätzungen olympischer Medaillengewinne. *Sportwissenschaft*, *38*, 131–148.

[19] Raab, M., & Philippen, P. (2008). Auf der Suche nach der Einfachheit in Vorhersagemodellen im Sport. *Sportwissenschaft*, *38*(4), 131–148.

[20] Matsuzawa, T. (Ed.). (2008). *Primate Origins of Human Cognition and Behavior*. New York: Springer Publisher.

[21] Cardinali, L., et al. (2009). Tool-use induces morphological updating of the body schema. *Curr. Biol.*, *19*, R478–R479. https://doi.org/10.1016/j.cub.2009.05.009.

[22] Matavita, A., & Irika, A. (2004). Tools for the (body) schema. *Trends Cogn. Sci.*, *8*, 79–86.

[23] https://langint.pri.kyoto-u.ac.jp/ai/index.html.

[24] Wilke, A., & Barrett, H. C. (2009). The hot hand phenomenon as a cognitive adaptation to clumped resources. *Evol. Hum. Behav.*, *30*, 161–169.

[25] Rosenbaum, D. A., Chapman, K. M., Coelho, C. J., Gong, L., & Studenka, B. E. (2013). Choosing actions. *Front. Psychol.*, *4*, 273. https://doi.org/10.3389/fpsyg.2013.00273.

[26] Weigelt, M., & Schack, T. (2010). The development of end-state comfort planning in preschool children. *Exp. Psychol.*, *57*, 476–482. https://doi.org/10.1027/1618-3169/a000059.

[27] Elisabeth Pacherie on Motor Intentionality Newen, A., De Bruin, L., & Gallagher, S. (Eds.). (2018). *The Oxford Handbook of 4E Cognition* (pp. 369–387). Oxford, UK: Oxford Press.

[28] Orasanu, J., Connolly, T., & Calderwood, R. (1993). The reinvention of decision-making. In G. Klein, J. Orasanu, & C. Zsambok (Eds.), *Decision-Making in Action: Models and Methods* (pp. 3–20). Norwood, NJ: Ablex.

[29] Tversky, A., & Kahneman, D. (1981). The framing of decisions and the psychology of choice. *Science*, *211*, 453–458.

CHAPTER TWELVE

How to cope with uncertainty in COVID-19 times

In the heat of the coronavirus crisis, in which COVID-19 is shutting down most of the world's standard behavior, this chapter was written on the first day after Angela Merkel, the German Federal Chancellor, announced a new set of rules that increased regulations after weeks of many public and private institutions and businesses, such as schools, daycares, restaurants, and some shops, already being closed. Until this moment, the 16 states of Germany had been setting their own rules for how strict or loose they wanted to be, with some allowing restaurants to stay open and others closing them. Even within a state, some cities (e.g., Cologne) had stricter rules than others (e.g., Düsseldorf). On March 22, Merkel and all 16 state presidents had a video conference to establish one set of rules for all people in Germany. The decision was made when Germany had 22,672 identified cases and 92 deaths, and the tragedy unfolding in other European countries painted a picture of horror (Fig. 1, right side for worldwide death toll of 14,641 on March 23, 2020). In an effort to slow the spread of the virus, one of the rules meant to reduce contact between people outside their immediate family or household was the banning of gatherings of two or more people.

How do governments decide on the basis of expert opinions and the data provided, also whether the banning of gatherings is enough to reduce the spread of the virus? Would it be better to be strict and ban traveling to and from work for sectors that are less important (as the Italians have done) or movement outside the house entirely other than seeking medical attention or supplies or food (as the Spanish have done), or should we calculate that gathering with two or four people will not make much of a difference to hospitals' capacity to cope with the virus? How can we measure if a set of rules is effective in the following weeks, given the incubation period of the virus is up to 2 weeks? One rationale behind any of the decisions being made was to slow the rate of new infections to reduce overload on the healthcare system and to gain time to develop treatments and a vaccine. But how do we predict the future growth of a virus when so many factors are influencing the dynamics of such a pandemic crisis?

Judgment, Decision-Making, and Embodied Choices
https://doi.org/10.1016/B978-0-12-823523-2.00012-X

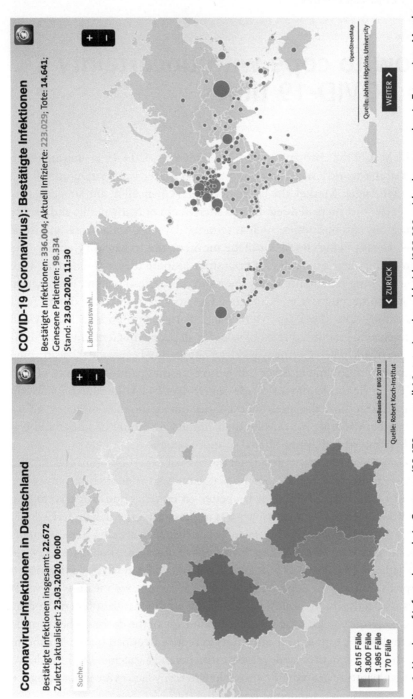

Fig. 1 Number of infected people in Germany (22,672 across all 16 states) and worldwide (223,029, with a large number in Europe) on March 23, 2020. *(Used with permission from Tagesschau).*

The growth rate indicates the number of new infections and deaths. It is currently exponential, meaning that, for example, in about a few days the number of infections doubles. Growth rates (i.e., how quickly infections doubled) varied on that day in Europe between 1 and 10 days. Of course, many factors influence this rate and that is why it is hard to compare such numbers between countries without knowing multiple factors, such as concomitant illness of the patients, treatments offered, and what mitigating actions countries have taken (from almost full shut-downs to almost free movement).

The test for the virus can produce so-called false-negatives, that is, a negative result when in fact the tested individual does have the virus. Given that in some countries these tests are self-administered in the current crisis, results may be less reliable. In addition, the infection rate is dependent on the number of tests conducted, which varied on March 20, for example, between more than 300,000 (South Korea, $N = 316,664$) and less than 500 (Ukraine, $N = 316$), but at that moment in time, there was a linear correlation between the number of tests conducted and the number of confirmed cases: the more tests conducted in a country, the more cases found. It is of course also evident that it is not only the total number of infections, deaths, or tests that is important but also these numbers need to be related to the number of inhabitants, and rates may vary dramatically depending on whether you are looking at the data for, say, India or the Faeroe Islands. Averaging numbers, as well, is not always meaningful; for example, COVID-19 is very harmful for elderly people and those with a weak immune system, and the patients who overload the hospital system are those who need intensive care and lung ventilators (the virus affects the lungs and can result in death when the lungs cannot produce enough oxygen).

Around the world, the heated debate over how much action is to be taken is going on, but most agree that long-term predictions are almost impossible to make given the dynamics of the situation we are facing since March 2020. My colleague and former boss Gerd Gigerenzer from the Max Planck Institute of Human Development in Berlin, Germany, suggested that an important lesson to be learned from this outbreak is the need to improve risk literacy [1]. In the same vein, Peter Gøtzsche, director of the Institute for Scientific Freedom in Copenhagen, Denmark, asked what would have happened if the Chinese had not tested their patients for coronavirus: "Would we have carried on with our lives, without restrictions, not worrying about some deaths here and there among old people, which we see every winter? I think so" (p. 1) [2]. What would happen if we did not ignore base rates and understood that some of the deaths would have occurred with or without the pandemic, as Juan Gervas [3] from Madrid, a quite heavily hit city in Spain, reported on March 14, 2020:

> In these people, elderly, sick men, the mortality is probably not extraordinary, but rather the one that "is expected", the one that would have occurred anyway, with or without the pandemic. Its impact on mortality is meaningless. It is impossible to notice its impact without the news because the number of cases and deaths are irrelevant in a world in which millions of people die each year (and half of them due to hunger and wars) (p. 1).

The statistics in March 2020 showing the average mortality of various countries as argued earlier are misleading for many reasons, as neither personal nor contextual factors are considered. An extreme case of this is the Italian data [4]. These data show that actually 99% of the patients who died from COVID-19 had a comorbidity and an average age of 80 years. These national and international examples from reliable scientific data sources (let us not talk about fake news and unreliable data) highlight that it is not easy to make fast choices on the individual or societal level. It is thus not surprising that well-respected statisticians are arguing that we need to prepare not to overreact to multiple developments, as John Ioannidis of Stanford University suggested [5]. What exactly does this mean for the decisions our leaders are making regarding how many people can gather in public or whether it is best to close all or some of the shops in a country? I can only repeat that we need to cope with that uncertainty, increase risk literacy, and make a personal choice depending on our own personal factors and the context in which we all live.

How do we now rate the actions of governments regarding health measures for society and individuals?

The simple answer is to use valid information and make an individual judgment of what risk-group you belong to. Given people cope differently with uncertainty, this is a very personal decision. For society the balance between different interest of a free society and how it functions best as well as the health security of risk-groups is at end a political decision that is informed by science. Currently, most virologists when asked how the virus will develop and when we will have medical countermeasures respond quite carefully and base their answers on knowledge of previous viruses, as they cannot predict how this new virus will act. Whether governments or individuals are overreacting or underreacting can only be answered in hindsight.

For the government of Italy, this has indeed been a traumatic experience given that the country has been the hardest hit in Europe. As of March 23, 2020, the infections were at a high of 59,138 and 5476 deaths were recorded—about 800 a day over the preceding weekend. Why did Italy have extremely larger numbers than compared with other countries? It has been suggested that country-specific factors have played a role, such as the mean age of the population being older or a lower number of intensive care beds with lung ventilators, among others [6]. As argued earlier, in hindsight it is easy to say we should have prepared better, knowing that the data from China indicated a growing epidemic, but the risk was perceived as low that a similar situation would arise in Europe. Because the virus moved in Europe at different times and speeds, in March 2020 it seems that many countries are prepared for the pandemic to grow but this preparedness will not stop the virus fully. Most likely, as experts predict and the reader will know when reading these lines, we will reach herd immunity, preventing the virus from moving further, when 60%–70% of citizens have been infected, and hopefully less 1% of the population (most likely the very old and those with weakened immune systems) have died.

For the individual, risk taking may depend on one's age or health conditions and the strength of the immune system. However, on a societal level, even young and healthy people have been asked not to gather in public places in an effort to "flatten the curve," so as to avoid a peak number of severe infections overwhelming the healthcare system. As the Bavarian state president Markus Söder put it, we may save not only those who follow the rules but also those who did not. In a previous chapter, I also talked not only about underreactions but also about overreactions, as happened after the 9/11 terrorist attacks, when in the United States there were about 1500 more car accident fatalities than in previous years because many people avoided flights and took long road trips instead, putting a much higher number of cars on the streets and highways.

In addition to learning to cope with uncertainty, we should strive to understand the risk of base rate neglect, as explained in previous chapters, to be prepared for similar events in the future. Many decisions must be made for a particular point in time, as the coronavirus crisis demonstrates, and may not even be valid for more than a few days or weeks, so they need to be dynamic. Whether the opportunity costs of banning social contact and shutting down a country, and its economy are acceptable is also a moral question.

With the decisions facing individuals and governments dealing with the coronavirus pandemic, moral decisions as evaluated by thought experiments such as the trolley dilemma discussed in an earlier chapter—in which a person is asked to decide whether the loss of one life is an acceptable price to pay for the good of a larger group, society, or mankind—take on new relevance. Ending on a more positive note, I see an outpouring of social support, positive effects on the environment, and useful changes in the way we work and educate people (remotely) around the world. In my own home city of Cologne, I have never before experienced quite such an atmosphere.

References

[1] G. Gigerenzer, https://www.project-syndicate.org/commentary/greater-risk-literacy-can-reduce-coronavirus-fear-by-gerd-gigerenzer-2020-03, 2020 Retrieved 24 March 2020.

[2] P.C. Gøtzsche, Are we the victims of mass panic?, BMJ (2020) https://www.bmj.com/content/368/bmj.m800/rr-1 368:m800. (Published 6 March 2020).

[3] J. Gervas, Fighting coronavirus (Covid-19) pandemic. First, do not harm, https://www.actasanitaria.com/fighting-coronavirus-covid-19-pandemic-first-do-not-harm/, 2020.

[4] Italian COVID-19 Surveillance Group, Report in Corvid-19, (20 March 2020)

[5] J.P.A. Ioannidis, A Fiasco in the Making? As the Coronavirus Pandemic Takes Hold, We Are Making Decisions Without Reliable Data, STAT, 17 March 2020, pp. 1–11.

[6] R. Porcheddu, C. Serra, D. Kelvin, N. Kelvin, S. Rubino, Similarity in case fatality rates (CFR) of COVID-19/SARS-COV-2 in Italy and China. J. Infect. Dev. Ctries. 14 (2020) 125–128, https://doi.org/10.3855/jidc.12600.

CHAPTER THIRTEEN

Ten statements for simplifying your life with embodied choices

In the following, I have summarized the previous chapters in the form of 10 statements that can be used as a guide to apply embodied choices in everyday life. This chapter tries to contextualize the empirical findings from the previous chapters using real-life examples in the domains of health, work, sports, and relationships. Many of the choices refer to routine decision-making and subjectively important choices we make as individuals, groups, or societies. The main message is to use the information provided in this book to simplify your personal life with embodied choices that can be applied to your own context. As argued earlier, the book is not meant to be used like a recipe that needs to be followed exactly to produce a great dish. Rather the information about judgment and decision-making and specifically about embodied choices is meant to be information that you can use for your own satisfaction, no more and no less.

#1: Choices are embodied choices

I argued earlier that choices are not pure cognitive processes but include your emotions and your body. Listening to your current feelings and your bodily responses helps you to trust your choices. Whether your gut is full may influence the way you make a decision. Do you remember my spaghetti Bolognese example, with which I opened the first chapter? This is an example of a subjective choice based on personal preferences—there is no right or wrong answer to the question of whether I should have spaghetti Bolognese today if I just had it yesterday. Such choices are embodied choices because the body can signal what we need, and sometimes we need to control those signals that have evolved. The basic tenet of the first rule is to trust your gut feelings. If you are an expert in something, your myriad experiences are somehow used in your body to inform you and you should listen. It may therefore be quite important that your choices reflect whether you decide intuitively or deliberately, with a full or an empty stomach.

How can we contextualize this statement? Charles Darwin (Chapter 1, Fig. 3) married his cousin Emma after producing a table of pros and cons but in the end trusted his intuition. I assume readers have made important decisions in their lives, whether forming relationships, deciding what to study, or figuring out how to achieve goals at work. The rule to trust your intuition can be applied to those decisions with which you have experience. Thus you may be better off relying on your intuition than writing down the pros and cons as Darwin first did before he followed his intuition.

#2: Choices are governed by a less-is-more strategy

The belief that less of something is better than more of that thing seems to be supported by research. Try to use only a few but valid pieces of information when making choices. Try to generate only a few ideas or options when you have experience in that domain. Use simple heuristics such as Take-The-Best, using the first piece of information that distinguishes between two options to make a choice. Use Take-The-First to trust the first idea you generate in a domain you know about. Simple heuristics as explained in Chapter 2 are based on the principle that less is more, whether you choose between given options or generate options yourself. The simplest of these heuristics, the recognition heuristic, has been explained in Chapter 2 with the example of the popular television game show "Who Wants to Be a Millionaire," in which only one of four options is correct and allows the player to move to the next level of the game. Which city has more inhabitants, Kyoto or Fukuoka? Most people recognize Kyoto as the right answer because larger cities appear more often in news and on the Internet. Following the recognition heuristic allows you to make fast but good decisions—in experimental tasks and in real-life strategies, such as devising an investment plan.

How can we contextualize this statement? Consider choices in which options are given and try to sort the information in the order of the options' validity. Use only the information that discriminates between the two or more options to make a choice. If you instead generate new ideas, do not try to generate all the options you can come up with but stop after a few and select the first generated.

#3: Choices are grounded in your movements

Choices regarding abstract concepts such as time can be influenced by your current position or movement of your body. Remember the example in Chapter 4 about moving a meeting? Does "next week's Wednesday meeting is moved forward by two days" mean the meeting will take place on Monday or Friday? The answer is likely to be influenced by moving forward or backward when answering this question. Choices are embodied and influenced not only by your gut, as indicated in Chapter 1, but also by your current posture, movement direction, or hand movements.

How can we contextualize this statement? Think about how to use your memory when thinking about your past or future. Studies discussed in Chapter 2 suggested using your movements to activate a memory that is stored in your body. To recall something from your past, lean back to bodily "travel" in that direction; to think about your future, lean forward. Likewise, positive feelings are associated in your body with upward movements and sad feelings with downward movements. If you need to pay strict attention to a task you might slow the pace of your breathing, which increases heart-rate variability and produces activation of the parasympathetic system you need for those tasks. If you are a student or teacher, use movements to anchor memory to the body; remember how moving your fingers on an imaginary keypad can help you to remember your bank account PIN or other important code. The advantage is not limited to numbers: For example, it has been suggested that learning vocabulary or facts for your next exam can be supported by movement-related memory strategies.

#4: Actions enable perception and cognition

By moving through space, as when an outfielder catches a baseball, we enable our perception to functionally work. An athlete does not need much cognition to predict where the ball may land. Jay Gould, introduced in Chapter 5, called this physical intelligence, and I call it motor intentionality. We may be tricked by perceptual illusions but as soon we act, our actions are likely to reduce the illusion. You may remember the study about being less likely to choose an advertised product when we have oral interference (e.g., eating popcorn or chewing a gum; Chapter 5, Fig. 3). The effects were described in Chapter 5 for other senses too, such as touch. Finally, environmental factors influence your choices, such as higher temperatures making you more impulsive, and may change your moral decision-making.

How can we contextualize this statement? Move when you want to allow your perception to work functionally. When temperatures rise, make sure that you remember that the choice you make may be influenced by impulsivity and if the situation allows you to delay the decision, make it in the cooler evening. Financial risk is perceived differently depending on your gut feelings. Consider the risks of your financial choices under different conditions of satiety and temperature.

#5: Decisions are influenced by your long-term movement history

Do you remember from Chapter 6 that judges in gymnastics who could perform a movement in their own athletic career judged the movements of gymnasts better than their counterparts who had not produced that movement themselves? It seems that observing movements of others is a way of using our own motor system to simulate the movements we observe with our own body. This potential of our motor system helps not only to control movements but to predict, estimate, and interpret movements of others has many social implications, from judging sport movements to making neurological diagnoses to making judgments based on empathy processes, to name a few—even esthetic judgments. You may remember the paper titled "I can, I do and so I like" that summarized nicely that our own long-term movement history affects our perceptions, emotions, and cognitions when observing actors, pictures, movies, and other people and things associated with the arts. And these effects are not limited to vision: Recall, how I was moved to purchase a picture of a bench in New York's Washington Square that I saw in the Metropolitan Museum of Art after sitting on a bench in that same park. Sounds, too, can have a huge impact on aesthetic judgments and have societal relevance as well: Manufacturers have been required to add running sounds to otherwise silent electric cars to warn people when cars are approaching.

How can we contextualize this statement? When making decisions that seem to be unrelated to your own movement history, reflect on the information from Chapter 7. Maybe sports decisions, aesthetic judgments, and choices based on empathy may be more strongly related to our long-term movement history than we thought.

#6: Choices in the real environment can change the impact of the body

Long-term consequences of our choices are often unembodied. In Chapter 7, I talked about medical choices, shopping choices, and liking people or objects. It is hard to act to prevent long-term consequences that are not felt strongly enough, such as climate change or the risk of COVID-19 infection. Making healthy food decisions is not easy when shops have the sweets stacked in front of you as you wait for the cashier. In Chapter 7, I also talked about how so-called fast-and-frugal trees can make many real-life decisions easier, and how your posture and that of people you observe can influence how much you like a person or thing. These preference judgments and first impressions may be correct. In Chapter 7, examples showed that more deliberation, that is, more thinking about your choices, does not make your decisions automatically better.

How can we contextualize this statement? For medical decisions, use information that is valid, as the previous chapters on simple heuristics claim, use fast-and-frugal trees, and understand base rates or other information provided by reliable sources. When shopping, remember that arm position and current bodily processes can influence your choices. Push your shopping cart with straight arms when approaching the checkout lane where all the sweet things are. Eat first and then go shopping. Try to provide bodily contact with things you wanted to change, such as bringing politicians to see the plastic in the ocean before they make decisions in meetings.

#7: Embodied choices are individualized and culture dependent

In Chapter 8, I asked if women and left-handers have better intuition, to illustrate that individual differences you cannot change can alter your choices. The same argument was used for cultural choices. Do you remember when I talked about why left-handers have an advantage in sports such as fencing and tennis, and why they are perceived differently when gesturing during talks? Or do you remember the study about nonverbal communication showing that women read facial expressions of emotions better than their male counterparts? Judgments based on individual differences matter, and some of these individual factors can be trained, as was demonstrated in Chapter 8 in studies on higher cognitive functions, creativity, and problem-solving, among others.

How can we contextualize this statement? Gestures are not only the product of thinking but also can influence your thinking. If you gesture with your right hand you may be better perceived by an audience of mostly right-handers. Observe your posture and gestures to find out how you feel about things and use what you learn to improve your thinking. Remember how Mark Zuckerberg, cofounder and CEO of Facebook, and Steve Jobs, the late cofounder of Apple, used walking meetings to promote creativity and problem-solving.

#8: First-time choices can be made embodied

In Chapter 9, I illustrated that first-time choices are tough, as we cannot rely on our experiences for that specific choice. I gave as examples the first time voting, the first time considering climate change actions, and the first time being faced with a particular moral decision. It seems that for these choices, activating feelings that are related to the choices to be made is important. In the climate example, touching waste in the ocean may have more of an impact on behavior than sitting at home and thinking about the climate. In Chapter 9 (Fig. 1), it seemed as well that washing one's hands produces more volunteering. Whether the increased hand washing that people are practicing during the COVID-19 pandemic that I discussed in Chapter 12 will produce such a positive effect is unknown at the time of this writing. If it occurs it may not be possible to determine if the cause was the hand washing or some other factor, such as the feeling of solidarity that has been observed in many societies. The COVID-19 pandemic reveals at the same time that even experienced stakeholders in societies have a very hard time in making decisions when such an event is perceived as unique.

How can we contextualize this statement? First-time choices are often perceived as hard to make. If you have no experience and no information, making a choice is almost like tossing a coin. Try to increase exploration and your experience in these situations. If first-time choices are important, you may need to buy time and information and learn to trust your feelings.

#9: Embodied choices are tuned by evolution

In Chapter 10, I argued that evolution shaped our embodied choices. Most of our higher cognitive functions such as reading and speaking are most likely rooted in the sensorimotor system. Gesture communication is much older than the verbal communication we use today. The use of simple tools we needed to survive by making fire or hunting efficiently and the creative thinking that arose from using these tools may have been shaped by evolution. Even the simplest organisms such as the bacterium *Escherichia coli* with the most basic sensorimotor system and no brain seems to make quite impressive choices to survive. Animals such as the Caledonian crow I mentioned in Chapter 10 produce striking solutions to problems and some animals even outperform humans on some tasks. Neuroscience has made new discoveries about how the motor system is involved in language understanding and production; for example, if the motor system is impaired, action words are more affected than nouns in speech production. I also cited Andy Clark, who indicated that our representation of the world comes about by acting in the world. Evolution shaped us to survive in changing environments and our body and our movements are the central interface with that environment.

How can we contextualize this statement? Well, evolution shaped our embodied choices and can be contextualized to any situation. I think, however, that we may need to accept with humility that our higher cognitive functions are based on very simple processes and that other animals may need a different treatment.

#10: Embodied choices can be trained

In Chapters 1–10, I tried to provide enough evidence and arguments to support the idea that choices are indeed embodied. The body and its current and past movements influence almost all of our behavior and the processes we often frame as perception, cognition, emotion, or something else. The given examples span very different kinds of choices in distinct domains, ranging from highly individual to large-scale societal decisions. In Chapter 11, I argued that embodied choices can be learned. One way to trust your intuitions and the bodily information is to learn implicitly. Do you remember the example I gave of how we learn our first language implicitly but any additional languages more explicitly? Or how Rich Masters from New Zealand showed that if you learn implicitly and are under stress you perform better and your working memory is not overloaded? These are just two examples of the need to create playful situations in which people can learn things without verbalizing and let the system gather information that later can be used for intuitive choices or gut feelings. Another way to improve such learning that uses embodied choices is time-pressure or dual tasking, as in both cases our so-called cognitive system does not interfere.

How can we contextualize this statement? Often, we do not have time to consider and wait for options. Trust your intuitions in these situations and use simple heuristics, as they are often built for these time-sensitive situations. If possible use implicit learning tools to make later decisions intuitive such that they become embodied.

Index

Note: Page numbers followed by *f* indicate figures.

A

Actions, 52–53
Alien hand syndrome, 99
Allen robot, 19
Analogy instruction, 126
Anterior cruciate ligament (ACL) injury, 11–12
Anxiety disorders, 115
Attentional dot-probe task, 3–4
Autonomic nervous system, 39–40

B

Body choices, 121–122
Botox, 99
Brain damage from accidents, 101–102
Brain-gut behavior connection, 3–4

C

Catching fly balls, 47–48
CCU. *See* Coronary care unit (CCU)
Chinese room, 17–18, 18*f*
Choice evolution, 119–120
Climate choices, 114–115
Cognitive analysis, 59–60
Cognitive deficits, 101
Cognitive functions, 88–94
Cognitive performance, 61
Cognitive psychology, 120
Cognitive system, 151
Conceptualization perspective, 16–17
Conservative Party, 113–114
Constitution perspective, 20
Context, in decision making, 37–38
Coronary care unit (CCU), 77–78
Cortisol, 35
Court decision, 35–36, 42–43
COVID-19, 139, 150
    false-negatives, 141
    growth rate, 141
    health measures, 142–144

infected people in Germany, 139, 140*f*
infection rate, 141
Italy, infections in, 143
statistics in March 2020, 142
Cue validity, 11

D

Dancing movements, 52–53
Decision making, in sports, 70–71
Decision-specific reinvestment scale, 39
Decision table, 6, 6*f*
Dictator game, 107
Downward movements, 30–31
Duplo test, 54–55

E

ELDERMET project, 41
Elections, 80–81
Embodied aesthetics, 67–68
Embodied choices, 145–146
    body conditions influence in
        downward movements, 30–31
        facial feedback, 32–34
        handedness, 30
        hands and fingers, 30–31
        left and right movements, 32
    definition of, 2–3
    in educational settings, 126–127, 127*f*
    esthetic, 67–68
    in finance, 106–109
    first-time choices, 150
    gut feelings, 3–7, 35–38
    in health, 103–106
    implicit learning, 134–135
    influenced by environment, 58–61
    learning, 127–129
    during multitasking, 94–97
    sounds and, 68–70
    sports outcomes, 129–130
    tool use in, 130–133, 131*f*

Embodied choices *(Continued)*
  touch, 72–73
  vestibular signals, 72–73
  women and left-handers intuition, 87–88
Embodied cognition
  definition of, 13
  sensorimotor theory, 20
Empathy, 52–53
End-state comfort effect, 132–133
Escherichia coli, 120–121, 150–151
Esthetic choice, 81–82
Esthetic embodied choices, 67–68
Exercise effect, 92–93
Expertise effects, 66, 70–71
Eye-tracking cameras, 72

F

Facial feedback, 32–34
False-negatives, 141
Fast-and-frugal trees, 78, 148–149
Fast heuristics, 10
Fear of missing out (FOMO), 97
Finance
  embodied choices in, 106–109
  risk, 147–148
First-time choices, 150
Focal dystonia, 98–99
FOMO. *See* Fear of missing out (FOMO)

G

Gestures, 29–30, 149–151
Giant hand effect, 100
Grasping, 130–131
Green Party, 113–114
Gross domestic product, 130
Gut feelings, in embodied choices, 3–7,
    35–38
  and brain work, 38–41
  in decisions changes, 38–41
  in risky behavior, 41–43
Gymnastics, 65–66

H

Handbook, 17–18
Handedness, 30
HDPI. *See* Heart Disease Predictive
    Instrument (HDPI)

Health, embodied choices in, 103–106
Heart Disease Predictive Instrument
    (HDPI), 77–78
High-stakes decisions, 74–75
Hogarth's concept, 125–126
Holistic approach, 119
Hot choice, 61
Human microbiome project, 41
Human motor system, 122–123
Hypothesis testing, 125–126

I

Ice climbing task, 128
Illusion, 48–51
Implicit learning, 125–126, 134–135
Individual and cultural differences, 85,
    87–109
Intelligence tests, 91
Intuitive reasoning task, 37
Intuitive thinking, 125

L

Language choices, 119, 122–123, 122*f*
Liking people, 80–81
Logistic regression function, 77–78
Love hormone/bonding hormone.
    See Oxytocin
Lucky rookie effect, 129

M

Medical decisions, 77–79
Metaanalysis, 115
Metaphors, 115–116, 126
Mirror neurons, 54–55
Monetary value, 82*f*
Moon perception, 48–49, 49*f*
Moral choices, 115–116, 116*f*
Moral decisions, influenced by temperature,
    60–61
Motor intentionality, 56
Motor interference, 95
Motor system, 148
Movement
  acoustic information of, 69–70
  experience, 66
  in high-stakes decisions, 74–75

influence our emotional judgments, 32–34
   sounds, 68–69
Müller-Lyer illusion, 49–50, 50*f*
Multitasking, 94–97

N
Neuroscience, 150–151

O
Overconfidence, 95–96
Oxytocin, 51

P
Parasympathetic system, 39–40, 147
Phantom pain, 99–100
Physical intelligence, 147
Power pose, 22–23
Primate Research Center, 131
Probiotics, 39
Problem-solving, 91–93

R
Recognition heuristic, 10–11
Remote associate test (RAT), 88
Replacement perspective, 18–19
Robot Soccer World Cup (RoboCup), 19
Rubber hand illusion, 99–100
Rules of thumb, 9

S
Self-control, 90–91, 104–105
Sense-model-plan-act, 19
Sensorimotor system, 36–37
Sensorimotor theory, 20
Shakey's task, 19
Shopping choices, 148–149
Shopping decisions, 79–80, 80*f*
Simple heuristics, 9–10
Situated choices, 119
Social Democrats, 113–114
Social exchanges, 107

Social interactions, 52–56, 59–60
Sounds, 68–70
Stress hormone, 35
Sunlight, 18–19

T
Take-The-Best heuristics, 146
Take-The-First heuristic, 70–71, 71*f*
Temporal parietal junction (TPJ), 68–69
#TheDress, 16
Thinking outside the box, 88
Time choices, 127
Time pressure, 151
TMS. *See* Transcranial magnetic stimulation (TMS)
Touch, 73
TPJ. *See* Temporal parietal junction (TPJ)
Transcranial magnetic stimulation (TMS), 66, 68–69
Trier Social Stress test, 74
Trolley dilemma, 60–61
Trust games, 107–108
Turing test, 17–18

U
Ultimatum game, 108

V
Vagus nerve connections, 39, 40*f*
Ventral pathway, 102
Vestibular signals, 72–73
Vision choice, 47–48

W
Walk and talk, 88–89
Walking meetings, 89–90
Water jar problem, 85, 86*f*
Weighted-additive strategy, 6
White-coated experts, 74
Women and left-handers intuition, 87–88

Y
Yips, 97–99